ALIENS AMONG US
Exploring Past and Present

ALIENS
AMONG US
EXPLORING PAST AND PRESENT

Schiffer Publishing Ltd

4880 Lower Valley Road • Atglen, PA 19310

DEDICATION

As you venture along your life path, you meet some people with amazing abilities. Connie and I were led to two such individuals in Salt Lake City: K and Doc Kivett. They introduced us to communicating with the spirit world using a channeling board. Without these two people, this book would not have been possible. In spite of physical problems that would decimate most people, these two individuals never fail to inspire with their sense of humor and outgoing personalities. God was very generous when he led us to them.

When I started to write this book, my first project was to convince myself that aliens really existed. When our guides introduced us to the spirit of Mou, an alien spirit, our understanding of the visitors around us increased by light years. His presence has been an immense influence on this book and me personally. It seems only fair that he be included in this dedication.

My wife Connie has been my soulmate and calming influence for over fifty years. If I had told her that we would be communicating with alien spirits before we got married, I can only imagine her reaction. Our journey together has truly been blessed, and hopefully it will continue for many more years.

EPIGRAPH

While channeling with the spirit of my alien friend, Mou, I asked him if he had one message for humans, what it would be. He answered:

*We are only here to help you. Just because you
do not see us does not mean we are not here. There are
many things you do not see that are around you. We are
one of them and in fact we walk among you.*

Front Cover Image of crop circle by Lucy Pringle

Designed by Matt Goodman
Type set in Futura & Times

ISBN: 978-0-7643-5006-1
Printed in China

Published by Schiffer Publishing, Ltd.
4880 Lower Valley Road
Atglen, PA 19310
Phone: (610) 593-1777; Fax: (610) 593-2002
E-mail: Info@schifferbooks.com

For our complete selection of fine books on this and related subjects, please visit our website at www.schifferbooks.com. You may also write for a free catalog.

This book may be purchased from the publisher. Please try your bookstore first.

We are always looking for people to write books on new and related subjects. If you have an idea for a book, please contact us at proposals@schifferbooks.com.

Schiffer Publishing's titles are available at special discounts for bulk purchases for sales promotions or premiums. Special editions, including personalized covers, corporate imprints, and excerpts can be created in large quantities for special needs. For more information, contact the publisher.

CONTENTS

ALIENS ARE AMONG US

You are about to embark on a unique way of learning about the world of extraterrestrial visitors. In this book I use our gift of spirit communication to investigate the presence of extraterrestrial beings and their unidentified flying objects that move them from place to place here on Earth and around the galaxy. The words of the spirits are stated exactly as they were received with no alteration. Every quote by the spirits is recorded on video and audio as proof of the event.

OPEN AND READY

One evening during a channeling session, I asked my guide why they selected us to make all this information available, and he replied:

We tell you things because
you are open and ready.

It is my hope that you are also open and ready to hear the truth about visitors not of our planet. This book contains information never before introduced to the general public and I hope you accept it as I have, with an open mind.

We've learned that aliens have souls that exhibit the same spirit energy as humans. In addition, they have access to the same realms in Heaven occupied by *Homo sapiens* souls. Once you accept these facts, the miracle of spirit communication has unlimited potential. As unbelievable as it may sound, we have communicated directly with an alien spirit named Mou from far outside our Solar System. We have asked him many questions and his answers will test your imagination as they tested ours. There is a chapter that tells the stories of various personal encounters that have involved me—complete with pictures. You might be surprised to find out that things you thought were just unusual, were really alien occurrences.

I show you pictorial evidence of UFOs dating more than 12,000 years ago, I talk about the truth regarding what happened in Roswell, New Mexico, a cover up concerning the events in Rendlesham Forest in Great Britain, ancient alien structures, and information concerning alien abductions. One chapter is dedicated to the statements of famous people, including two Presidents of the United States who have actually personally viewed UFOs.

You will become more informed about the true role, and often extreme practices, conducted by the governments of the world in keeping the truth about aliens from the people. More intriguing than the fact that they go to excessive measures to maintain the lie, is the reason why the extraterrestrials are kept a "dirty little secret."

A WELL-ORDERED GALAXY

As you become more aware that aliens actually exist, I will introduce you to a concept that not only do they come from all parts of the universe, but that they have been here on our planet a lot longer than humans. In fact, their cultures are so advanced that they outgrew the need to kill one another. They are governed efficiently by a Galactic Commission and are responsible for much of the learning associated with the progress of man here on Earth. Not only do they mean us no harm, they are here to observe and lend a little help.

You will see that the possibility of communication with the spirit presence of an alien really does exist as we establish an ongoing conversation with an alien spirit. I fully realize that it will take a little while for that last statement to sink in, but if you continue to read the following chapters, you will learn the answers to many of the mysteries of our galaxy and beyond.

I have also included a chapter on biblical references to extraterrestrials. Many are familiar with Ezekiel's Wheel, but there are numerous other references. The destruction of Sodom and Gomorrah has been attributed to alien intervention, but the guides have provided the truth to what really happened. In addition, they even tell us the truth about the Star of David that led the wise men to the baby Jesus.

THE BIG SKY

The scale of the universe is unimaginable. There are 10 to the 22nd power stars in our visible universe. That means 10 with 21 zeros. For comparison, this equates to approximately all the grains of sand on earth. Our own galaxy, the Milky Way, has from 200 to 400 billion stars. That would roughly equate to the number of grains of sand to fill one Olympic-sized swimming pool. In one of our sessions, we were told that we have only seen five percent of the universe. The odds of life outside our Solar System is overwhelming. As you will learn, there is much more going on out there and here on Earth than we've ever imagined.

Life in the late 1940s and 1950s was relatively simple as I grew up in a rural area of Pennsylvania. As a child I remember laying on the grass at night and looking at all the stars in the Heavens. I always took it for granted that God or a master Deity created everything I was viewing. When I looked at the night sky, I remember wondering if there really were aliens that traveled the vast expanses. (Keep in mind that, at this time, we had not set foot on the moon and Buck Rodgers was state of the art.) In those days, I could find the Big Dipper and Orion but never really thought there would be travelers from a foreign world visiting us here on Earth.

WAR OF THE WORLDS

Our communication companies have instilled a fear of aliens since the use of radio to reach the masses. My parents spoke of a radio show that took place before I was born called "War of the Worlds" that struck panic in many people who tuned in. It was broadcast in 1938 and narrated by Orson Welles. Planned as a Halloween broadcast and aired in news format, the show told of an attack on our world by Martians. Panic swept the country until people realized it was only a radio show. Some even committed suicide. Apparently the presence of aliens would be an event to be feared by all. My childish imagination had no way of understanding what it would really mean if an extraterrestrial ship would land in our backyard.

COLD WAR PROMOTES SPACE TRAVEL

Space travel by humans became a reality as the United States and Russia fought a cold war during the 1960s and 1970s that always seemed to have a chance of open conflict. Russia beat us into space, but we showed *them* by being the first to put a man on the moon. Technology grew exponentially and our ability to communicate knew no bounds. As we communicated more easily, I became aware of more conversation concerning the existence of aliens. It seemed as though the sighting of strange flying objects and weird happenings, like crop circles, were more common than previously imagined. It was even whispered that an alien craft had crashed in *far-off* New Mexico! I never thought much about it because our Government at the time told the public the incident was nothing more than a weather balloon. In those days, I was naïve enough to believe our government would never deliberately lie to its citizens.

Television gave the average citizen the opportunity to watch a variety of events from around the world. Shows began to tell of adventures of space travelers outside our Solar System. Movies like *Star Wars* seemed to make the existence of alien beings a fact that was taken for granted. More people could recognize Han Solo than the President of the United States. In spite of sightings and strange happenings in all areas of the world, governments vehemently continued to state that the existence of alien life was a myth. At the same time our government was so emphatic about aliens being a figment of people's imaginations, the military was investigating reported occurrences through an operation called Project Blue Book.

THE TRUTH IS OUT THERE

For many years, I watched the television show *The X-Files* whose opening sequence always ended with the phrase "the truth is out there." While I had no doubt that the truth concerning extraterrestrials was out there, somewhere, access to accurate information was almost impossible to find. The American government certainly had no interest in providing the truth and, as you will see, has gone to great lengths to keep the truth from the public. Not only is information suppressed on this side of the Atlantic, but many other countries also actively suppress information on UFOs. In one of our sessions we were told the real reason why governments around the world go to such lengths to keep the presence of extraterrestrials a secret. I think the true reason will surprise you.

There are literally thousands of Internet websites dealing with aliens, but it is nearly impossible to separate truth from fiction. There are even interviews by former astronauts Gordon Cooper Jr. and Edgar Mitchell detailing encounters with strange flying objects. A chapter in this book is dedicated to very reputable individuals who have gone public about seeing strange flying objects. I find it inconceivable that individuals of this stature would jeopardize their reputations by telling lies about their encounters with the unknown. Our spirit informants will comment on whether they were seeing optical illusions or not.

Television shows, such as *Ancient Aliens* on the History Channel, highlight intricate structures created thousands of years ago. Many of the structures, such as the pyramids of Egypt, seem to suggest an ulterior motive in their alignments with the heavens. Fortresses in Peru were built to such intricate detail that the stones seem to have been cast in place, not cut with primitive tools. The pattern of stone structures in Stonehenge, England, has defied the imagination for many generations. Crop circles occur around the world and there is no logical proof of how they are constructed and why no person or vehicle has been observed creating one. Something certainly seems to have been out there for a very long time, but how can anyone ever find the truth? Heavenly guides will always tell the truth, so we will ask them!

COMMUNICATING WITH HEAVENLY GUIDES

Our gift of spirit communication has given us a unique opportunity to ask the heavenly guides about a huge variety of subjects. If you have read my previous book, *Afterlife: What Really Happens on the Other Side*, you will have an understanding of the afterlife and the amazing ability of the spirit guides to supply answers, no matter what the subject. They seem to occupy a dimension where there is access to all information: past, present, and future. Why not ask a spirit, not of this dimension, about beings, not of this earth?

For those of you not familiar with the term "spirit guide," here is a short explanation:

> A guide is a spiritual being that devotes their existence to helping others. All of us have personal guides that help us with our daily lives. Their messages can come as words you hear in your mind or maybe what you think is your conscience speaking to you.
>
> There are master guides that generally devote their time to carrying out God's work. In addition to the master guides, there are lower-level spirit guides that help an individual along their life path. There are guides present from the time you are in the womb to your time of passing. As you will also find out, there are also guides that are not part of the human species.

In this book, I ask the spirit guides for answers regarding the entire spectrum of questions concerning our visitors from another area of our Solar System. Their answers will often astound you, but I believe all cases reflect the truth. The truth really is out there; you just have to know who to ask.

We receive the messages from the guides by means of a channeling or spirit board. Their words are spelled out one letter at a time, transcribed on paper, and recorded on video and audio. The exact words of the guides are printed in blue type in this book. Trust me, there are

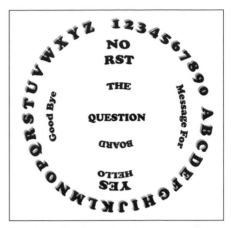

The channeling board used to communicate with the human and alien spirits. Courtesy author.

many messages in this book that you will find very hard to believe. Please don't shoot the messenger—literally or figuratively. I am passing on the messages as they were given to me; you can accept them or not. In any event, they will give you something to think about.

As I mentioned, the key for this direct communication with the spirit guides is a channeling board. Not to be confused with a Ouija Board, the Spirit Board we use has been designed to reduce the possibility of evil spirits making an appearance and distorting our messages. In contrast to other boards, our design features a glass top that protects the board and provides a smooth surface. Instead of the classic planchet, we utilize a shot glass. That's right, I said a shot glass! We each place a finger on the shot glass and the glass on glass surface makes it easier for the spirits to deliver their messages. My wife Connie generally takes notes, so we can clarify answers and keep the session on track. The video and audio records are maintained if the need arises to review what was recorded.

This channeling technique was taught to us by our friends in Salt Lake City. For three generations K and Doc Kivett at the Ninth House Bookstore, located at 3443 South State Street, have been interpreting the messages of the spirit guides. Their father designed a talking board, like the one pictured here, and they have been receiving messages on it for almost forty years. K's mother, the late Carol Greene, founded the Ray of Light Research Center. Their research work concerning the metaphysical and spiritual dimension has gained worldwide recognition. We have actually refined our channeling technique to the point that we use Skype so our friends can be in Salt Lake City with the board and we are in front of our computers in Pennsylvania. Most of the sessions with our alien spirit, Mou, were actually conducted long distance. Our spirit guides love technological innovation. The guides are the ones that suggested we use Skype!

It is my opinion that the aliens want us aware of their presence, so that cooperation will become easier in the future. I also think they want to give us messages about how we are killing ourselves by eating unnatural foods, polluting the air, damaging the ecosystem of the planet and waging wars.

ACCEPTING THAT ALIENS EXIST

Once a person accepts the concept that aliens exist, it opens the door to many other questions. We will explore where they come from, how many varieties of aliens exist, what they look like, whether they have souls, and where they go when they die. We will discover how long they have been on this planet and why they are here.

Throughout this book you will see information derived from when we channel with the soul of an actual alien. The information given by his spirit will stretch your imagination to new limits. He is very forthcoming in his answers and we will even discuss the longevity of the human race compared to the life span of our neighbors on other planets in other Solar Systems.

CHAPTER 1

ALIENS DO EXIST

When my daughters heard that I was writing a book about aliens, they thought it was a really bad idea. My youngest daughter even threatened to get married so she could change her last name. It seems as though they both share the belief that anyone supporting the theory of the existence of extraterrestrials has one foot in an insane asylum. I must admit, I considered writing the book under an assumed name—that of my youngest daughter! (My wife thought that was really a bad idea.)

Since the heavenly guides have decided to give me the information, the least I can do is print the truth as they have offered to us. In the words of Admiral Perry during the War of 1812: "Damn the torpedoes, full speed ahead." Another saying that comes to mind is: "The truth will set you free." In spite of the fact that some of the information incriminates many, I am going to publish the statements just as given to me by the spirit messengers.

We did discover that different guides had access to different types of information. When I started to gather my research, it never occurred to me that the guides would put me into contact with the spirit of an actual alien. It was only after this contact that certain information became available. Apparently, the guides of human spirits answered the questions to the best of their abilities, as *they* have observed it. You will see that our conversations with an extraterrestrial boosted our knowledge to an entirely new level.

At some time, I cannot believe that everyone has not gazed into the sky and wondered if there was life on other planets. From my initial comments, I am sure most of you have already anticipated the answer to the title of this chapter. If the answer was "no," this would be one of the shortest books ever written. Have no fear; there are many pages to go as I try to investigate all aspects of finding the truth about our visitors from other dimensions or worlds.

One evening, in July 2012, we conducted a private channeling session where I wanted to investigate extraterrestrials. On that particular evening, I requested a master guide that was familiar with aliens and a guide named Phillip joined us for the evening on the spirit board. I started the session by asking if aliens exist at this time on earth. He replied:

They have frequented the earth, yes.

We were definitely on the right track. My follow-up question asked if there were any aliens among us at the present time and our guide replied:

At any given time.

That answer certainly covered all the bases and, as I was to learn, was an understatement. I exhaled a sigh of relief; the future of my new book was assured! My next question inquired as to what purpose was served by aliens. His answer caught me by surprise but made sense:

They are the watchdogs of the universe.

As we were to find out later, as our sources of information increased, Phillip was quite accurate in his assessment of their role. I think you will find the true extent of this quite amazing. When you think of aliens, the word "benefactor" does not usually come to mind.

It seems like there are an awful lot of alien sightings, especially when you surf the Internet. When I asked if there was currently an increase in alien activity, the answer was:

It has always been active.

I read on a website that sightings increase before times of crisis or disaster, so I inquired whether extraterrestrial activity increased before times of natural disasters. He kind of ducked the question when he answered:

Give or take.

With all the bad stuff going on in the world, no wonder alien activity has increased; there is an awful lot to watch. Whenever you see aliens in the movies or on television, they seem to be quite violent and they are often seen blowing things up. I thought this might be a good time to pursue whether extraterrestrials are something to be feared.

I asked if they have any ties to the demonic. Phillip answered:

No.

When I asked if they meant any harm to humans the answer was also:

No.

At least we were getting off to a pretty positive start: they were simply watchdogs that meant us no harm. As our abilities to communicate with the other side increased, we were to find out that they not only mean us no harm, but in many instances, served a positive function. I inquired if they were concerned with the battle of good over evil and the answer was once again:

No.

That was kind of disappointing, but as we learned, they are primarily observers; however, there are times that they get involved to save us from ourselves. Thinking I would get right to the point, I asked what their desire was for the human race. The guide's answer was:

There is no concern. They are merely observers and occasionally lend an idea or two.

The way he was ducking the question, it was beginning to sound more and more like our politicians in Washington. I realized he was not talking about our members of Congress when the guide said they generated an idea or two.

GOD CREATED EVERYTHING

I asked whether aliens were God's creation. His answer was:

Hard to explain. They were here before our Lord.

This statement concerning the presence of aliens before the birth of Christ will be well documented in Chapter 2 in which I show you images of flying saucers dating to as early as 17,000 years BC. As you will see in Chapter 3, there are numerous references to aliens in both the Old and New Testament. Our guide seemed to be having a tough time with the answers concerning the creation of extraterrestrials, so I posed the question: Did God create the extraterrestrials? After a pause, he answered:

God created the universe and they are part of the universe.

As you are about to find out, God created life on other planets long before he let human life evolve on Earth. In later sessions, I asked Mou, our alien spirit, about the role of aliens in the evolution of the Earth; he said the following:

We have aided in many ways from your beginning.
Your sciences did not put mankind on earth soon enough.
They are some 50,000 years late.

In another session, he pointed out just how instrumental aliens were in possibly preserving life on Earth when our scientists tested a hydrogen bomb.

I know we sent advisors to teach young scientists
about atom splitting. You figured out hydrogen. You made a
bomb and you were warned not to. You set it off and just
about destroyed Earth. We had to stop it.

Not only do aliens exist, they have helped humans when they seem hell-bent on destruction, like playing with explosive toys they don't fully understand. Mou clarified just how long there has been an alien presence:

You have to remember we have been here when
three man-like animals roamed the planet. We watched
your last Ice Age. We have let your planet evolve with
only two or three major intrusions.

In another session, he mentioned that they were here since the time of the dinosaurs. They have been visiting our planet since long before humans decided to stand up straight and go for a walk.

WHERE DO ALIENS COME FROM?

If you are starting to believe in aliens, it is only natural to wonder where they come from. When I started, I thought extraterrestrial visitors would be from within our Solar System. Maybe there was some truth in the old wives tale about a man from Mars, so I inquired if they were from one of our known planets. Mou's reply was:

Not known. The planet is unknown to man.

In this day of modern astronomy and huge telescopes, it seems almost inconceivable that there is a planet in our Solar System that remains unknown to man. What went over my head was that fact that the planet was unknown because it was from outside our Solar System. When I asked how many planets in the Milky Way support intelligent life, Mou answered:

Thousands.

With thousands of planets supporting intelligent life, it is a wonder there are not more aliens than humans on our planet. In my research on the Internet, I read something about a hollow planet theory. When I asked if there was any truth to the theory his answer was:

If you mean Earth, no.

(I will investigate the hollow planet theory later in this book.) It seems from reports of people who have observed UFOs that the extraterrestrial vehicles are only seen part of the time. Eyewitnesses say that the ships seem to just disappear. One explanation would be that they simply accelerate so fast the eye loses contact with the vehicle. I asked the guide why the ships are only seen part of the time. His answer was:

Most UFOs are from different dimensions.

While it is true that some aliens occupy other dimensions, there is another reason why we cannot see their ships. In a subsequent interview, when I asked Mou why his ships were invisible to humans, he gave me another answer.

We just go stealth. We have shown your scientists the simple form of this. We change an electron force so light goes through us. We are there; you just cannot detect us.

According to our alien friend, it seems they have the ability to switch from our visual dimension to one that is unseen at will. As you will see in a future chapter, this stealth concept will also help to explain crop circles appearing without any evidence of an alien vehicle. It certainly undermines the old concept that "seeing is believing."

THE EXISTENCE OF NIBIRU

Is it possible there is a planet out there that is hollow and could house alien life without any detection? In November 2012, we questioned master guide Phillip about the existence of an unknown planet in our Solar System named Nibiru. When asked if it exists, his answer was:

Yes.

For those of you not familiar with Nibiru, Zecharia Sitchin, in his book *The Twelfth Planet*, proposed an explanation for the origin of human life that involved ancient astronauts. He stated that there was a race of aliens from a planet beyond Neptune called Nibiru. This supposed planet has an elliptical orbit in our Solar System. Some calamity folks think there will be a cataclysmic event when Nibiru has a near impact with Earth. I asked the guide if the aliens were from Nibiru. After all that background information his answer was a somewhat anticlimactic.

No.

I followed up by asking if it would be a risk for earth to which he answered:

It is being carefully watched.

Note that once again he ducked the answer. When asked if astronomers were keeping the presence of Nibiru a secret the answer was:

Yes.

Next, I asked if we should take precautions and he answered:

Nothing different.

According to the guides, there really is an unknown planet out there named Nibiru but it does not portend Armageddon here on Earth.

WHAT DO ALIENS LOOK LIKE?

My guess is that our government knows exactly what an alien looks like. I asked our guide if the extraterrestrials looked anything like the gray forms that are portrayed on television and motion pictures. His answer was:

No.

Next, I asked the direct question: What do they look like? He was a bit evasive when he answered:

All different types.

I could tell it was not going to be easy finding out what our visitors from outer space looked like or where they came from. Next I asked if they looked anything like humans. His answer was:

No. Let us say they are quiet observers.

I have no idea what he meant by this statement, but it was becoming obvious that there would be no direct answer as to their appearance by this guide. It was not until we made contact with our alien spirit that we received substantive information about their appearances. He in fact turned out to be tall, skinny, with big eyes, and bluish skin.

Before leaving the subject on that evening, I made one more attempt: Do the extraterrestrials want to keep their identity hidden? The reply was:

They do. However some will be more viewable.

There was no way Phillip was going to spill the beans and tell me what the aliens looked like. As you will see, in Chapter 10, Mou actually describes himself and some of his friends. Judging from their evasive answers, I think all the master guides went to law school!

BACK TO THE FUTURE!

On another evening, we communicated with a master guide named Valentine. As a guide, Valentine brings a religious point of view, since he is an assistant to the Saints. He will prove to supply accurate information, but it is limited by his experiences. I thought I would ask him some of the unanswered questions. I started out by stating that we were told that aliens observe and report. Who do they report to? His answer was:

Their source in a future time.

Take special note that our guide mentioned "in a future time" in his answer. At the time of the session, the answer went over my head. As it turned out, the answer is actually the key to the origin of some of our alien visitors. This will be clarified in Chapter 7, when we discuss the events at Roswell, New Mexico.

I kept thinking about our interplanetary friends reporting on the actions of humans, so I asked the purpose of the reports that were made by the extraterrestrials. His reply was:

They are as much fascinated with
Earth as humans are with them.

This comment proved to be extremely accurate. They have been studying humans since the beginning of human evolution. Next I asked how many types of aliens exist. Valentine's reply was:

They come and go. Hard to speculate.

I would assume from that answer that there are quite a few different types of visitors. As I write this chapter, the bar scene in *Star Wars* comes to mind with all the different creatures. You will learn that in the case of the appearance of aliens, the truth really is more strange than fiction.

PERSONAL PHOTOGRAPHS

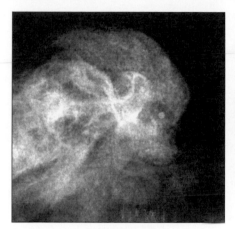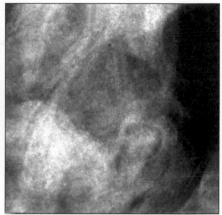

An energy mist in the shape of a very strange creature. Courtesy author

An energy mist in the form of Star Wars' Chewbacca. Courtesy author.

One night I was photographing on the Gettysburg Battlefield in Pennsylvania, and took a picture of an energy cloud that actually resembled Chewbacca from *Star Wars*. When I photographed the image, I could not see the form with my eyes. It was only captured with flash on the camera.

Various descriptions of extraterrestrials have been given by individuals who have suffered alien abductions. One description portrays the visitors from outer space as having small reptilian, gray bodies with oversized heads and bulbous black eyes. When I asked Valentine if this description was accurate, he answered:

Yes, cross between humans and animals.

I have included another picture of an energy cloud that seems to be a cross between a human and an animal. Once again, I could not see the image with my eyes and it was only picked up with the camera flash. Whether it is alien related or not, the image does not look overly friendly, especially when you are taking pictures by yourself in the dark.

ANIMAL MUTILATIONS

Another mystery that is found in all parts of the world is the presence of animal mutilations. When the carcasses are found, they display surgical-like precision incisions, where portions of the bodies are removed. Generally, areas of the faces of the animals are taken. There seems to be no rhyme or reason to the mutilations and the carcasses are not eaten by other animals or carrion creatures. When I asked our alien guide the reason for the mutilations, he replied:

> *DNA testing. We want to see how*
> *much you are killing yourselves.*

The watchdogs from outer space don't appear to be too happy with the way we are treating Mother Earth and what we are doing to our food supply. What appears to be a senseless mutilation of animals is really a scientific method for finding what toxins are present in our food chain. This testing is all part of their watchdog of the universe role.

CENSORED SUBJECT

Moving on to a subject discussed by abductees, I asked if there were aliens breeding with humans. I think I embarrassed Valentine, a messenger of the Saints, because his answer was:

> *I would rather not discuss.*
> *Some things are removed from God's plan.*

I will leave you to fill in the blanks on this one! Our conversations with the alien Mou tells of the results of inbreeding, but that is for another chapter. When I asked if the visitors wanted to change the genetic structure of the human race he answered:

> *Vice versa.*

I interpreted this to mean that our governments are attempting to alter human genetic structure to incorporate alien characteristics. This testing of genes during the 1940s resulted in problems realized in current generations (also a topic for future chapters).

I had read somewhere that you could stop an abduction by repeating the Lord's Prayer over and over. When I asked our guide about that, his reply was:

> *In most cases it would serve the same*
> *result as being abducted by a human. No.*

I guess if you have been selected for abduction, there is little you can do about it.

From our conversations with the guides, we know that:
• Aliens are among us.
• Extraterrestrials have been here since before our Lord.
• Aliens are the watchdogs of the universe.
• Visitors from outer space watch and observe the human race and report their findings.
• Occasionally, aliens abduct humans for study and sometimes place implants in their bodies. (There is a separate chapter devoted to the subject of abductions.)
• Most importantly, aliens do not mean us any harm.
• There are many different types of aliens and their appearances vary. (As we are about to learn, that is an understatement.)

This chapter contains an awful lot of information to absorb at one time. As the old saying goes, "You ain't seen nothing yet." We have also shown that there are many different types of extraterrestrials that are present on Earth at all times. Their role as watch dogs of the universe needs a little more investigation along with why they put implants in their abductions.

CHAPTER 2

GRAPHIC EVIDENCE OF ANCIENT ALIENS

H aving watched *Ancient Aliens* on television, my curiosity was aroused concerning how long extraterrestrials had been visiting the earth. When I asked the guide the question, his answer was:

*They have been here since
the beginning of time.*

Even the television show underestimated how long aliens have been visiting! While that includes the period before the evolution of man, if the statement is true, they were certainly present and probably had an influence on many of our early cultures. Programs on television depict structures and images that could not have possibly been constructed using the technology of the times. We had already been told that aliens visited the earth since the beginning of time. I want to show you evidence of the earliest record of them.

One evening I asked the guide if there were any other places where ancient aliens are mentioned. His reply was:

There are references in ancient drawings.

With that statement, I began to search for some of the earliest recorded images that could be interpreted as extraterrestrial. As I was to find out, there are some very unusual pictorial depictions of interplanetary visitors—far more than I realized. The guide was certainly correct when he said there were references in ancient drawings!

VISITORS 15,000 YEARS BEFORE CHRIST

It is generally assumed that writings in the Old Testament date to around 1500 BC. Cave images predate the Bible by over 15,000 years. One of the most ancient images occurs in cave paintings dating between 17000 BC and 15000 BC, give or take a couple of years. Located near Cabrerets, France, this image was found in the Pech Merle cave. As you can see, what appears to be saucer-shaped figures are being viewed by an individual. The individual seems to have a tail and multiple appendages. We were to learn that there are some really unusual looking creatures

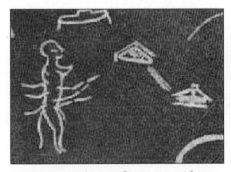

Cave painting showing flying saucers from 15,000 BC near Le Cabrerets, France. Public Domain.

Cave painting from 10,000 BC showing astronauts near Valcamonica, Italy. Public Domain.

that travel our universe—maybe this is one of them. I would certainly think this would qualify as an early reference to aliens.

Moving on in time, I found a cave painting, or pictograph, from Valcamonica, Italy, in the Lombardy Alps, that dates to around 10000 BC. It depicts two figures in what appears to be modern space suits. I would think that seeing something like this more than 10,000 years before the birth of Christ would make an impression on the residents of the period. The images seem non-typical of the other cave paintings of the era.

LITTLE WHITES

LONG TIME VISITORS

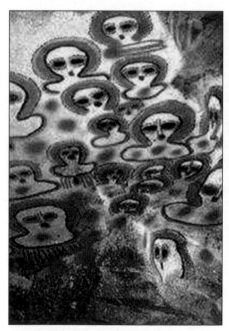

A ca. 8000 BC cave image showing "Little Whites" from France. Public Domain.

An image from Kimberly, Australia, showing "Little Whites" dating to 3000 BC. Public Domain.

The image on the left is what I believe to be one of the most amazing pictures and is from around 8000 BC, found in a cave in France. In this instance, the painting portrays faces very typical of the current visualizations we have for the "Little Whites." It also appears the artist saw quite a large group of the visitors.

Whatever these early humans saw, it made quite an impression on them. Thankfully, the images were painted in caves, so they were preserved for modern viewing.

For the sake of comparison, let us jump ahead in time about 5,000 years. Amazingly similar to the French cave paintings (page 30 photo on the right) was taken in a cave in Kimberly, Australia. This image was painted around 3000 BC, about 5,000 years later than the French painting. Once again, the figures resemble what we refer to as Little White aliens. The similarity in the two cave paintings is remarkable, considering the images occur half-way around the world from each other and were made by totally different cultures separated by 5 millennia. It is possible that the same type of extraterrestrials have been visiting all areas of the planet for a very long time.

ALIENS AND SAUCERS IN ALGERIA

Dating to 6000 BC near Tassili, Algeria. Note the flying saucer. Public Domain.

As I did my research, one thing that made an impression is the fact that the images exhibited a distinct similarity, no matter where they were located on our planet. Believe it or not, some of the best early cave paintings with alien inferences come from the Sahara Desert region of North Africa. Paintings near Tassili, a mountain range in Algeria, provide some very interesting images. Dating to 6000 BC, the cave painting has a figure with a head that could be a helmeted space suit. In addition, if you look in the upper right corner, you will see a detail that looks a lot like a saucer. Whatever inspired the early human who transcribed the picture, it is certainly non-typical of what we would ordinarily expect to see in the Sahara desert. This area of Africa has other images in caves that may indicate the alien presence, as well.

EXTRATERRESTRIALS IN PETROGLYPHS

There are many recorded images that can easily be construed as evidence of an alien presence in the American southwest. Since early Native Americans did not have the use of paper, they often displayed their art work by chipping images into stone. Being a resident of Utah, I photographed many examples of the Anasazi Indians throughout the red rock area of the state. They occupied the area from

Ca. 1000 AD, a form resembling a landing ship in Anasazi Canyon, Utah. Dollarphotoclub.

500 to 1300 AD. Around the fourteenth century, the entire Anasazi culture disappeared from the Southwest. What happened to their thriving communities is another mystery. Some say the aliens may have had something to do with their demise.

Many of the petroglyphs chiseled on the rocks or painted in caves seem quite out of place for the times. In some instances, they might be the result of an alien presence or influence. The image on your left was taken in Anasazi Canyon and contains several figures you would not expect to find in the typical early American Indian village. The form in the lower right corner looks like it could be some type of a landing ship.

Canyonlands National Park in southern Utah is one of the most remote and largest parks in the country. It covers over 527 square miles with many areas nearly inaccessible. Horseshoe Canyon contains an area known as the Great Gallery, the location of some of the finest petroglyphs in North America. Many

of the images are life-sized and contain very intricate detail. Pictured here, I have chosen an image known as the "Ghost Panel." The center image is very large in size and not what you would think to view in early Native American Indian culture. It is also surrounded by shrouded figures that add to the mystery of the image.

The most famous set of images in Canyonlands is named appropriately

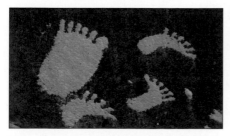

Feet with six toes on Newspaper rock in Canyonlands National Park, Utah. Dollarphotoclub.

Strange images dating ca. 1,000 AD in Canyonlands National Park, Utah. Dreamstime.

Newspaper Rock. Pictured at the bottom of page 32 is a small segment of the many images showing feet. You don't have to look too closely to realize that the feet have six toes on each foot. I am not sure if aliens have six toes, but it certainly becomes food for thought. We can be relatively sure that the Indians who carved these feet did not have the above-noted physical appearance.

Petroglyphs appear in all areas of the world. Halfway around the globe in Thailand and dating to around 2000 BC, there is more evidence of stone paintings that may indicate interaction with visitors from outer space. The paintings on rock panels certainly bear a resemblance to a group of "Grays." The guides told us our ancient visitors were anxious to learn about our entire planet and traveled to all parts to view the varied primitive cultures.

Rock paintings dating to 2000 BC of "Grays" from Thailand. Dollarphotoclub.

ALIENS IN FINE ART

Flying ships on an oil painting in Kosovo, Yugoslavia, dating to 1300 AD. Public Domain.

Not only do extraterrestrials appear in cave paintings and petroglyphs, they also appear in famous works of art. The Visoki Decani Monastery in Kosovo, Yugoslavia, dates to the 1300s. Located behind the alter, you will find a large, three-paneled mural that depicts the crucifixion of Christ. If you look closely at the upper right and left corners of the painting, you will find what looks like individuals in very strange flying machines. Art experts that attempt to debunk the alien theory point out that many religious works in the Byzantine style depict the sun and the moon, often with a human face or figure. I will let you decide for yourself if the images

A flying saucer in the 1500s oil painting *Madonna with Saint Giovannino.* Public Domain.

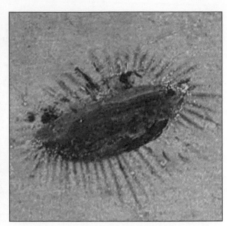

A close-up of the Madonna saucer. Public Domain.

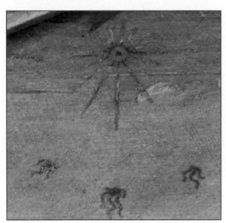

Unusual figures in the Madonna oil. Public Domain.

remind you of the sun or moon. I think we can all agree that the figures are a bit bizarre.

A very interesting work of art is currently located in the Plazzo Vecchio, the town hall of Florence, Italy. Entitled the *Madonna with Saint Giovannino,* the work is unsigned but attributed to Domenico Ghirlandaio, an artist who painted in the fifteenth century. What makes this oil painting interesting to extraterrestrial theorists is that over Mary's left shoulder you will find a disk-shaped object glowing in the sky. While there may be other explanations, the object looks a great deal like a flying saucer. The image top right shows a close up of the flying machine. You will note a distinct similarity to modern descriptions of flying saucers. If the artist wanted to depict the sun, I would think he might have made the image round. The oil painting also includes a man and his dog looking up at the object in the sky. I would also point out that men do not often look directly at the sun.

Part of the same oil painting, if you look in the upper left portion of the sky you will see three other unusual objects. In the photo at the bottom left, you will see a close-up of that area of the image. I believe the top part of the picture depicts the sun, but I have no idea what the artist had in mind for the three figures that

The Annunciation saucer. Public Domain.

A saucer with an energy beam in the 1486 oil painting *Annunciation of St. Emidius.* Public Domain.

seem to be floating in the air. (Keep in mind this was painted in the 1300s and everything that was viewed in the sky would have been thought of as a religious event.) In this case, the artist seems to have combined an alien sighting with the image of the mother of Jesus.

Another interesting fine-art image with alien implications is located at the Fitzwilliam Museum in Cambridge, United Kingdom. Entitled *The Baptism of Christ*, it dates to around 1710 and shows Christ being baptized by Saint

A saucer shaped vehicle with energy beam in the 1710 oil painting *The Baptism of Christ*. Public Domain.

John with a group of people looking on. The intriguing part of the image is the two figures being brilliantly lit by a ray of light that is being emitted from what appears to be a flying saucer. I am not aware that the early eighteenth-century artists were familiar with the concept of science fiction.

Dating to 1486, the art work *Annunciation with St. Emidius* depicts the same type of illumination from an object in the sky that seems to be some type of a saucer-shaped vehicle. The great work of art was painted by Carlo Crivelli. As seen in the enlargement on page 35 on the upper right, once again there is an illumination by some type of object, other than the sun. Ancient artists must have had visions that were unexplainable, but shown in their works of art.

HELICOPTERS IN ANCIENT EGYPT

A ceiling beam in Abydos, Egypt, showing modern flying machines created prior to 2000 BC. Dollarphotoclub.

Ancient Egypt is famous for its hieroglyphics, but none will appeal more to the alien theorist than those found on a ceiling beam in the town of Abydos. Located about 300 miles south of Cairo, the town contains archaeological remains from the first Dynasty through the thirtieth Dynasty. That is a long time, even for Egyptian history! It would seem that sometime during that period, the town may have had some alien visitors that impressed the carvers enough that the image is forever captured in stone.

In the upper center of the photograph, you will find what appears to be a modern helicopter, complete with tail and rotor. On the right, you will find a saucer-like image as well as what could be a larger vehicle. The bottom right image looks like a small plane with a large tail. On the left you will find what appears to be some type of winged object that has the landing skids from a modern helicopter. This single panel from thousands of years ago depicts objects we all recognize today.

There are many other examples of the presence of aliens throughout time here on Earth. In my research, I came to realize that not only is there a lot of visual evidence, but the drawings and images also indicate that there was not just one type of alien making an appearance. What we see is evidence of the many types of extraterrestrials from different areas of the galaxy. One can only imagine what early man thought when he first saw the strange visitors.

CHAPTER 3

BIBLICAL REFERENCES TO ALIENS

The Bible gives us an excellent narrative of the history of mankind for almost 4,000 years. Alien theorists are quick to point out that some of the actions described in the Old Testament were the work of aliens and not acts of God. As I continued to do research and communicate with the guides, I started to run across biblical references that had possible extraterrestrial implications. While I in no way claim to be a biblical scholar, I put together a list of specific verses that seemed to indicate the presence of ancient aliens. As you are about to find out, the heavenly guides were quite anxious to answer my questions, and some of the answers were quite informative.

The Holy Bible contains some of the earliest recorded histories of man, so it would be the logical place to search for their interaction with extraterrestrials.

DEATH OF THE ASSYRIAN ARMY

My first inquiry with the guide concerning specific biblical references quoted the book of Kings from the Old Testament. This book covers the period from approximately 960 BC to 560 BC, a period of 400 years. 2 Kings states:

> And this is what the LORD says about the king of Assyria: "His armies will not enter Jerusalem. They will not even shoot an arrow at it. They will not march outside its gates with their shields nor build banks of earth against its walls. That night the angel of the LORD went out and put to death a hundred and eighty-five thousand in the Assyrian camp."

My guess was that it would take an alien interaction to kill that many skilled fighters overnight without making a sound. All expectations were shattered when the answer from the guide was:

No.

Are you telling me that the death of 185,000 Assyrians was at the hands of an Angel commanded by God? His answer was short and to the point:

Yes.

There must be some very tough angels on the other side!

EZEKIEL'S WHEEL

I had read a chapter from Ezekiel of the Old Testament that seemed like a slam dunk for alien activity. This book covered the years 593 BC to 571 BC and told of his visions while exiled in Babylon. Ezekiel 1:1-28 refers to a great cloud with brightness, flashing fire. When I inquired if this verse dealt with alien activity. His answer was:

Yes.

The spirit guide finally agreed that a verse of scripture referred to an alien presence. His statement confirmed my belief that aliens were indeed recorded before the birth of Christ.

Ezekiel is one of the key references to a visit by extraterrestrials in the Bible. Sometimes these verses are referred to as Ezekiel's Wheel. If you read verses 4 through 28 closely, you can visualize a large alien mothership that dispatches multiple landing craft, perhaps similar to our modern helicopters with rotors that make a noise never heard before by the human witnesses. (As your read the verses, be aware that the author had never seen anything like alien crafts before and could only refer to the events in the vernacular of the time. The author would have been familiar with a wheel, but little else technologically.)

4. Then I looked, and behold, a whirlwind was coming out of the north, a great cloud with raging fire engulfing itself; and brightness was all around it and radiating out of its midst like the color of amber, out of the midst of the fire.

5. Also from within it came the likeness of four living creatures. And this was their appearance: they had the likeness of a man.

6. Each one had four faces, and each one had four wings.

7. Their legs were straight, and the soles of their feet were like the soles of calves' feet. They sparkled like the color of burnished bronze.

8. The hands of a man were under their wings on their four sides; and each of the four had faces and wings.

9. Their wings touched one another. The creatures did not turn when they went, but each one went straight forward.

10. As for the likeness of their faces, each had the face of a man; each of the four had the face of a lion on the right side, each of the four had the face of an ox on the left side, and each of the four had the face of an eagle.

11. Thus were their faces. Their wings stretched upward; two wings of each one touched one another, and two covered their bodies.

12. And each one went straight forward; they went wherever the spirit wanted to go, and they did not turn when they went.

13. As for the likeness of the living creatures, their appearance was like burning coals of fire, like the appearance of torches going back and forth among the living creatures. The fire was bright, and out of the fire went lightning.

14. And the living creatures ran back and forth, in appearance like a flash of lightning.

15. Now as I looked at the living creatures, behold, a wheel was on the earth beside each living creature with its four faces.

16. The appearance of the wheels and their workings was like the color of beryl, and all four had the same likeness. The appearance of their workings was, as it were, a wheel in the middle of a wheel.

17. When they moved, they went toward any one of four directions; they did not turn aside when they went.

18. As for their rims, they were so high they were awesome; and their rims were full of eyes, all around the four of them.

19. When the living creatures went, the wheels went beside them; and when the living creatures were lifted up from the earth, the wheels were lifted up.

20. Wherever the spirit wanted to go, they went, because there the spirit went; and the wheels were lifted together with them, for the spirit of the living creatures was in the wheels.

21. When those went, these went; when those stood, these stood; and when those were lifted up from the earth, the wheels were lifted up together with them, for the spirit of the living creatures was in the wheels.

22. The likeness of the firmament above the heads of the living creatures was like the color of an awesome crystal, stretched out over their heads.

23. And under the firmament their wings spread out straight, one toward another. Each one had two which covered one side, and each one had two which covered the other side of the body.

24. When they went, I heard the noise of their wings, like the noise of many waters, like the voice of the Almighty, a tumult like the noise of an army; and when they stood still, they let down their wings.

25. A voice came from above the firmament that was over their heads; whenever they stood, they let down their wings.

26. And above the firmament over their heads was the likeness of a throne, in appearance like a sapphire stone; on the likeness of the throne was a likeness with the appearance of a man high above it.

27. Also from the appearance of His waist and upward I saw, as it were, the color of amber with the appearance of fire all around within it; and from the appearance of His waist and downward I saw, as it were, the appearance of fire with brightness all around.

28. Like the appearance of a rainbow in a cloud on a rainy day, so was the appearance of the brightness all around it. This was the appearance of the likeness of the glory of the Lord.

There is a very detailed technical description that analyzes each verse on the website www.thelightside.org/EARSite/ears_ufos_biblefiles1.html, written by Jim Aho. He gives a very plausible explanation of what is taking place in each verse. I think you will find it worthwhile to check out this translation of what takes place in the biblical verses shown here.

BOOK OF ACTS

A similar quotation appears in the Book of Acts from the New Testament. Scholars believe the book was written around sixty years after the birth of Christ. Acts 14:11-12 reads:

And when the people saw what Paul had done, they lifted up their voices, saying in the speech of Lycaonia, The gods are come down to us in the likeness of men.

When I asked the guide if this verse was referring to aliens, his answer was:

No.

The answer was a bit of a disappointment; I really thought I was beginning to understand the biblical references.

NEPHILIM

The Nephilim were giants that walked the earth at the time the Israelites conquered Canaan. The best estimate is this took place from 1400–1350 BC. Alien theorists suggest the giants were of extraterrestrial origin. Some have hypothesized that they came from the planet Nibiru. They are referred to in the books of Genesis and Numbers.

Genesis 6:

The Nephilim were on the earth in those days, and also afterward, when the sons of God (bene Elohim) came in to the daughters of men, and they bore children to them. Those were the mighty men who were of old, men of renown.

Number 13:30–3:

The land through which we have gone, in spying it out, is a land that devours its inhabitants; and all the people whom we saw in it are men of great size.

I thought the Nephilim were prime candidates for proof of an alien presence, so I posed the question to a master guide, Saint Martin. His reply was direct and to the point:

No.

I was wrong again. My next question inquired if they were giants and he answered:

Early humans, large, yes.

What role did they play in the progress of man?

None in particular, like the dinosaur.

The rock images of Easter Island. Dollarphotoclub.

I thought I would switch subjects, so I pointed out that the Easter Island has the rock forms of 887 human-like figures. What is their significance?

Nephilims.

That answer caught me off guard, so I repeated myself: Are your saying the statues on the Easter Islands are modeled after the Nephilim mentioned in the Bible?

Yes.

So that is what the Nephilim looked like?

Yes.

Not exactly the information I was looking for, but at least I solved the mystery of the stone figures on the Easter Islands. Alien theorists have said they were the figures of aliens and only aliens could have formed the shapes. They never considered that a group of human-like giants could have moved the stones and fashioned them in their own likeness.

THE ANUNNAKI

Modern alien enthusiasts, thanks mostly the works of Zecharia Sitchin of Nibiru fame, consider the Anunnaki an ancient alien group of giants that came to Earth during the 3rd Millennium, BC, to the Sumerian or Mesopotamian culture in what is now Iraq. Stitchin stated that Anunnaki actually meant "those who from heaven came to Earth." His thesis states that the Anunnaki are actually from the planet Nibiru that passes by the earth every 3,600 years. If you recall, in Chapter 1 we discussed the planet Nibiru and the guide verified its existence.

The word Anunnaki actually does not appear in the Bible. Deuteronomy 2:10 refers to giants named the Anakites:

The Emites used to live there—a people strong and numerous, and as tall as the Anakites.

In addition, the Mesopotamian culture recognized the Anunnaki as gods; the issue is whether they were aliens.

When I asked the guide if the Nephilim, shown to be early humans earlier in the chapter, were the same as the Anunnaki, his answer was:

The Anunnaki of Mesopotamia.
Dollarphotoclub.

The Anunnaki shown with wings having the ability of flight. Dollarphotoclub.

Differences.

They were described as white gods from the skies. In addition, they were attributed with giving the Mesopotamians written languages, sciences, and building technology. When I asked if the Anunnaki were aliens our guide replied:

Yes.

There are many depictions in ancient Iraq of the Anunnaki appearing as giant figures with wings. I asked if they had the power of flight.

Of their own accord. Man has always been fascinated by flight.

According to the spirit guide, the Nephilim were early humans of very large size and the Anunnaki of Mesopotamia were aliens, at least some having the ability of flight. When our guides said there have been aliens since the beginning of time, they were apparently correct. Here we have more evidence dating back to 3500 BC.

Joel 2: 3–9:

The book of Joel in the Old Testament has a section that seems to describe a superhuman people who have the ability to create destruction and cannot be killed by the sword. I thought these verses were great candidates for alien references.

3. A fire devoureth before them; and behind them a flame burneth: the land is as the garden of Eden before them, and behind them a desolate wilderness; yea, and nothing shall escape them.

4. The appearance of them is as the appearance of horses; and as horsemen, so shall they run.

5. Like the noise of chariots on the tops of mountains shall they leap, like the noise of a flame of fire that devoureth the stubble, as a strong people set in battle array.

6. Before their face the people shall be much pained: all faces shall gather blackness.

7. They shall run like mighty men; they shall climb the wall like men of war; and they shall march every one on his ways, and they shall not break their ranks.

8. Neither shall one thrust another; they shall walk every one in his path: and when they fall upon the sword, they shall not be wounded.

9. They shall run to and fro in the city; they shall run upon the wall, they shall climb up upon the houses; they shall enter in at the windows like a thief.

When I asked our guide if this verse from Joel referred to an alien presence, his answer was:

Yes.

Another prime candidate comes in the Old Testament book of Zechariah when the prophet refers to seeing a flying roll.

Zechariah 5

Zechariah was a prophet from the Hebrew Bible who lived in Jerusalem from 520 to 518 BC. He is so emphatic in his description that he even includes the size of the flying object.

Then I turned, and lifted up mine eyes, and looked, and behold a flying roll. And he said unto me, What seest thou? And I answered, I see a flying roll; the length thereof is twenty cubits, and the breadth thereof ten cubits.

Keeping in mind that the vernacular of the time had no way to accurately describe what was being observed, the term "flying roll" could surely be an alien vehicle. When I asked the guide his answer was:

Yes.

The prophet Zechariah was observing the vehicle of an extraterrestrial and recorded it in a text that was to become the Old Testament of the Holy Bible. In this instance, a size and shape estimate is given for the vehicle. A cubit is generally estimated to be approximately eighteen inches, so the vehicle would be cylinder shaped, around thirty feet in length and fifteen feet in diameter. This description is similar to multiple modern sightings. It is unfortunate that the scribes of the time lacked the vocabulary to accurately describe what they were witnessing.

There are many other chapters in the Bible where modern scholars believe there is evidence of alien interaction. When I asked about the gospel of Revelations 9: 7-11, 1st Corinthians 15:40, and Genesis 28 that could be an alien abduction of Jacob, and others, the answer was in the negative. The guides are always quick to differentiate the acts of aliens with the miracles of God.

The Bible is a source of information about the visitation of extraterrestrials on our planet. It would be very interesting to know what alien information was included in the gospels that were not included in our existing Bible. I would suggest that the mention of aliens would have been enough reason to exclude the gospel from additional recognition.

THE STAR OF DAVID

While conducting our spirit interviews for this chapter, I found out some interesting information about two major events discussed in the Bible. When Christ was born, the three wise men were led to the baby Jesus by a bright star in the sky. I had read somewhere that maybe the bright star was actually an extraterrestrial ship that acted as a guiding light. I asked the guides if the Star of David was an alien vehicle. He replied:

It was a phase of Jupiter.

That answer caught me off guard so I said: "Are you telling me the Star of David was actually Jupiter?" His answer was:

Yes.

I find it amazing that the star lined up with Bethlehem in an accurate enough manner that they could locate the baby Jesus! With God, all things are possible.

SODOM AND GOMORRAH

I watched a television program that implied Sodom and Gomorrah were destroyed by alien space ships. Another presented the idea that the towns were destroyed when a large meteorite struck earth in the vicinity of the Alps. According to that program, a huge fire plume was created by the impact of the meteor that rose high in the air and fell to earth in the vicinity of the Dead Sea, the location of the cities of Sodom and Gomorrah. Scientists' core drilling in the glaciers around the world found layers of debris left in the ancient ice that indicates there was a cataclysmic event that occurred around 3250 BC, approximately the time of the destruction of the cities, adding credence to the meteorite theory.

One evening I decided to ask our master guide if alien activities caused the ancient destruction of the cities of Sodom and Gomorrah. His reply to the question was:

No.

When I asked if the destruction was caused by an asteroid hitting the earth, his answer was:

Coupled with an earthquake.

The television show was correct and in this case the alien theorists were wrong. Our guide verified the natural event that destroyed the cities as described in the Bible. Genesis 19:24 describes in biblical terms what happened to the cities:

Then the LORD caused to rain upon Sodom and upon Gomorrah brimstone and fire from the LORD out of heaven.

The biblical verse certainly describes the appearance of superheated lava falling from the sky to destroy anything in its path. Natural forces directed by God, not alien intervention, destroyed the cities of Sodom and Gomorrah.

Both the New and Old Testaments bear witness to the extraterrestrial events that were described by the scribes to the best of their abilities. As in most things, the Holy Bible is a pretty good starting place.

CHAPTER 4

ALIEN ARCHITECTURE

Throughout time ancient aliens have left evidence of their presence on the earth in the form of intricate designs or large structures generally built of rock blocks. Construction of these forms would challenge modern technology. These features date from long before the birth of Christ and would have required massive amounts of labor. They occur from Egypt to the Pacific Islands and South America. It is almost impossible to grasp the scope of these structures and images from photographs. It is also hard to understand how these features could be created with the tools of the ancients.

NAZCA LINES

When it comes to the size of the structures, it is hard to beat the Nazca lines and figures in South America. When seen from the air, the scale of the images is overwhelming, covering almost 300 square miles (around

An overview of the Nazca Lines of Peru. Dollarphotoclub.

450 square kilometers). That is an area equivalent to seventeen miles by seventeen miles!

The Nazca Lines are located in an arid Peruvian coastal plain located around 248 miles (400 kilometers) south of Lima, Peru. To view the line for yourself, insert S14 43 32.988 W75 8 54.996 into Google maps; you will be amazed to see the extent of the patterns for yourself.

The lines and figures date to between 500 BC to 500 AD and are either scratched in the ground or made by piling stones. Since this is an arid desert, the images have been preserved through the years. The shapes include flowers, a monkey, a strange creature with two human hands, one with only four fingers, a spider, and last, but not least, an astronaut. Most of the figures are located on a flat plain, but the astronaut is carved into a hillside.

Modern archaeologists have many theories concerning the Nazca lines, but up until now they have all been conjecture. When I asked Mou if he was familiar with the Peruvian lines his answer was:

Very.

I inquired whether the lines were the work of aliens and the reply was:

Yes.

Many of the theories concerning the lines hypothesize that the ancient residents worked in conjunction with aliens. When I asked if they assisted the local population, the answer was:

We just did it with our technology. It took three months.
It would have taken three generations if we let them make them.

So much for working with the local people. The formations were the sole product of alien technology and labor. I inquired as to the purpose of the different formations created by the lines.

Two fold. To give them a gift that they could see
when riding with us and a marking system that we
used to navigate from space. There are more around
the world not found. All a map for us.

One of the more interesting formations carved into the side of the mountain is a figure that could be the shape of an alien. When I asked the guide if the image represented a visitor from space, he said:

Yes, we were showing them
our weapons system. It will
blast rock or cut fine lines.
It is a magnetic laser.

An alien form in the Nazca Lines of Peru.
Dollarphotoclub.

I'd never heard any theory that the figure on the right was cut into the rock with a magnetic laser that was a type of weapon. Their technology 2,000 years ago was far more advanced than our modern weapons today. If their weapons were that accurate in those days so that they could carve precise figures into rocks using them, think what they must be able to do now...

In the photograph on the next page you can see the shape of a spider. Not only is the image quite large, but it is perfectly proportioned. It almost looks like the positioning of the stones had to be directed from an object flying overhead. (Keep in mind that the local Peruvian residents did not have access to flying machines in 500 BC.)

Of all the images in the Nazca lines, the spider stood out in my mind as one of the most unusual. It seemed to have no relationship to all the other images. When I asked Mou the significance of the spider, his answer was far from what I expected.

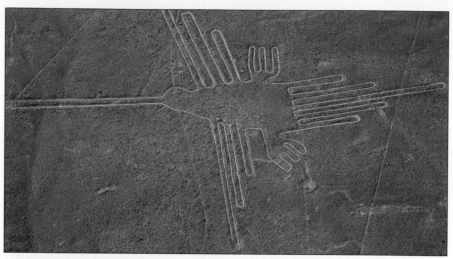

Another image from the Nazca lines, a hummingbird. Dollarphotoclub.

A huge spider from the Nazca images.
Dollarphotoclub.

That spider was what those aliens looked like. It is to honor the people of that time for accepting them.

This is the first time we were told that there are aliens in the shape of a spider! One can only imagine what thoughts went through the minds of the ancient Peruvian natives when they got their first glimpse of the oversized spiders getting out of the mother ship.

Another very interesting image that is part of the Nazca lines is the hummingbird. After learning the symbolism of the spider image, I could not wait to ask Mou what the hummingbird image stood for. His answer did not disappoint.

The wings are the landing area. If you do something pretty, the people remember. If you listen to the stories of the people, they will tell you who we are, why we come and where we went. You all need to listen to words passed down. Look at the art, it tells you there.

The ancient alien visitors wanted to be remembered by future generations, so they created the artistic geographic features that are now referred to as the Nazca Lines. It is only the closed minds of current generations that prevent the aliens' desire for recognition from being fulfilled.

The Nazca lines were designated as a UNESCO World Heritage Site in 1994.

PALPA FLAT MOUNTAIN

An overview of the Palpa flat mountain in Peru.
Dreamstime

If you don't think the aliens were busy enough in ancient Peru, a couple of miles from the Nazca lines near the town of Palpa, you will find a huge, flat-topped mountain. You can view this for yourself on Google maps by loading the coordinates -14.548961, -75.173963. It is difficult to get an idea of scale from the map, but this flat area is massive. In addition, there is no trace of debris from the material that would have to be moved to create such a level surface. As you can see, there is rugged terrain all around the flat area of the mountain.

My first question of the alien guide concerning the Palpa flat mountain was if the construction project was the work of aliens. His reply was:

Some, natural but embellished for landings.

When I asked further about its purpose, he said:

Another view of the Palpa flat mountain. Note there is no excavation debris. Dreamstime.

Landing place. A station to come and go and store fuel rods.

Having worked in construction for many years, I had some feel for the size and time it would take to excavate such a large area with modern earth-moving equipment. I asked Mou how long it took to flatten the mountain.

In a week.

It would take years to duplicate that effort today with our technology. Since there is no evidence of excavated material, I asked what they did with the waste material. He dropped another information bomb.

In the sea.

The sea is nowhere near the Palpa flat mountain! An obvious follow up would be to ask how they got it there.

We flew it there.

The flattening of the Palpa mountain is definitely a feat that defies our modern imagination. The combination of the Palpa flat mountain and the Nazca Lines are considered by many as proof that aliens were active contributors to the construction projects of the Peruvian residents around the beginning of the first millennium. Our friends on the other side have confirmed their beliefs and filled in many of the details.

CONE HEADS

Cone-shaped skulls from Peru. Dollarphotoclub.

Some alien theorists believe the extraterrestrials may have had cone-shaped heads. Local museums in the town of Ica display cone-shaped skulls that could either be those of aliens or humans who banded their skulls to resemble their alien helpers. When I asked Mou if the cone-headed skulls were aliens, his answer was:

Half breeds.

That answer needed a bit of follow up so I asked if he was saying that the skulls pictured on the left are those of humans bred with aliens. The reply was a simple:

Yes.

I figured I would rein in my curiosity and let the subject drop. In any event, the sheer scale and detail of the figures have been studied by archaeologists around the world.

PYRAMIDS OF GIZA

The last of the Seven Wonders of the World still standing are the Great Pyramids of Giza. The largest was completed in 2560 BC, stood 481 feet in height, and it is estimated that 2.3 million stone blocks, weighing between 2 and 15 tons each, were used in its construction. It covers 13.1 acres. The smaller pyramids were built for the Pharaoh's wives.

One of the Seven Wonders of the World, the Pyramids of Giza. Dollarphotoclub

It is not hard to believe that scholars would question how the ancient Egyptians would construct such a massive structure standing almost fifty stories high with heavy blocks without the use of cranes or other lifting equipment. It is estimated that construction took place over twenty years or 7,300 days. If 2.3 million blocks were placed over that time period, an average of 315 massive pieces of stone would have been cut, transported, and placed each day! A feat like this may not even be possible with modern tools.

It is not unreasonable to believe that the ancient Egyptians may have had some help in their endeavors, perhaps from extraterrestrials. In July of 2013, I began to inquire of the spirit guides if the pyramids were related to alien activity. The answer was:

Yes, pyramids encase energy.

I inquired what type of energy and the reply was:

Inert power.

The building of the pyramids was a massive project. Did extraterrestrial technology allow the building of the pyramids?

Yes.

The inside of the pyramids have complex passageways and chambers. I asked the guide the purpose of the interiors of the pyramids:

Burial chambers. Remember a triangle shape retains energy.

It seems inconceivable that the stones could have been lifted into place without some kind of supernatural assistance. I inquired if the aliens used an anti-matter device to lift the blocks. The answer put an end to that theory:

No.

How did they lift the blocks into place?

The lower portions came first. Used scaffold.

There are chambers and passageways in the pyramids that go so far underground, there is not enough oxygen to support human breathing or torches. There is a theory that the ancients had access to electricity. I asked the guide if the Egyptians had the use of electricity.

Yes, as did the Romans.

That was a bit of a bombshell! My next question was: How was the electricity generated?

I believe utilizing stones and iron.

Are you referring to creating a chemical reaction?

Yes.

They had to have light inside the passageway to perform the construction. I asked if they had electric lights in the passageways of the pyramids.

No.

As I was about to find out, sometimes the obvious is the correct answer. I asked how they lit the interior of the pyramids.

Daylight, some stones were left unplaced to allow light.

The pyramids appear to have been aligned to point to the stars in the constellation Orion's belt. I asked if there was any significance to the alignment of the pyramids.

*Back during that time there were mystics
who used the stars for insight.*

I was still unsure just what role the extraterrestrials played in the construction of the pyramids. Did the aliens provide the technological knowledge for the construction methods? The answer was:

The Mayan pyramid at Chichen Itza, Mexico. Note similarity to Egyptian Pyramids. Dollarphotoclub.

> *Yes, in many ways. They contribute to the mechanics.*

Did the aliens actually help in the physical construction?

> *Some of that and some by man.*

I figured that Mou could fill in some additional details about the pyramids, so I asked him when they were constructed.

> *1,000 years sooner to 500 years later. The first ones
> got sand buried so more came and then the kings wanted them
> as tombs and the last ones were needed for landing and
> storage. Then we started to use the sea.*

When I asked if the aliens still used the pyramids, his answer was:

> *Nope.*

The Myan and Aztec pyramids in South America resemble the Egyptian pyramids, so I asked if there was a relationship between the two. His answer confirmed my suspicions.

> *Same. UFOs. There is a big crystal missing
> from each to light up and guide us in.*

It seems as though the network of pyramids around the world had crystal beacons on top that lit up and acted as beacons to guide the UFOs on their flights around the Earth. That statement certainly solved a lot of theories about the purpose of the pyramids.

Pyramids around the world bear a striking resemblance. Pictured on page 58 is the Chichen Itza Mayan pyramid from central Mexico. You can see the similarity to the Egyptian pyramids. It is easy to imagine a giant crystal sitting on the top to guide the UFOs to a landing place. Pyramids can be found in Peru, Sudan, Iraq, Italy, and (would you believe?) the United States. A structure known as Monks Mound is found just north of East St. Louis, Illinois.

PUMA PUNKA

Intricate stone building blocks from the temple in Tiwanaku, Bolivia. Dollarphotoclub.

Puma Punka is a large temple complex, dating to around 600 AD, and located near Tiwanaku, Bolivia. The complex is constructed of large stone blocks, some weighing as much as 131 tons. Part of the mystery concerning the structure is that the large blocks of sandstone had to be transported up a steep incline from a quarry located a little over six miles (ten kilometers) away. Smaller blocks used for stone facing and carvings of andesite were transported from a site almost fifty-six miles (ninety kilometers) from the site. When I asked Mou how the ancients moved the huge stones, he indicated that the ancient cultures of South America were more technologically advanced than I'd imagined.

If you use magnetism, you can move skyscrapers.
If you put down a strip of magnets and put the opposing
force on the bottom you can move them by walking them in
place. The stones took longer to cut than to move.

In addition to the logistic problems involved with the construction, each block was cut to fine precision allowing the blocks to fit together with interlocking details, like a fine puzzle. Many of the joints are so precise, a razor blade will not fit between the stones. Such precision would require a very sophisticated understanding of cutting stones and an understanding of geometry far beyond the capabilities of the primitive civilization. Workmen today would be hard-pressed to cut the stones with such accuracy using modern techniques and laser measurements.

PUERTO DE HAYU MARCA

Puerta de Hayu Marca is translated in English as the Gate of the Gods. Located in Southern Peru near Lake Titicaca, you will find a huge door-like structure carved into the solid rock of the mountain. The doorway measures exactly twenty-three feet by twenty-three feet with a smaller alcove in the center of the base measuring just under six feet in height.

Native Indian legend tells that the carving is a "gateway to the lands of the Gods." They speak of it as a place where great heroes of the past passed through the gate to join their gods for a life of immortality. At times, these heroes even returned through the gate to inspect their lands.

When I asked the guides if the structure was created by aliens, his reply was:

Yes, a point of recognition.

Did aliens carve the doorway?

No, man did it to please us.

The residents must have enjoyed the alien presence and wanted to continue interaction with them. Mou gave me a little more clarification when I asked him the purpose of the structure.

To remind us to land there to visit. We had stopped and they
wanted to say come back. It works, we do come back.

The Hayu Marca structure in southern Peru. According to our guides, the site of an ancient wormhole portal. Dreamstime.

Remember the part where the legend said the portal was a gateway to the lands of the Gods? I asked Mou if it was really a portal. His answer reinforced the legend.

Nope, once a worm hole.

A wormhole entrance would have allowed the people or aliens of the time to enter and travel through time. In this instance, our alien friend confirmed the legends concerning the gateway to the Gods. The question, "are there any passageways behind the portal?" was answered:

Once.

Another legend tells of a sacred gold disk known as the "key of the gods of the seven rays" that had the ability to open the gate. There is actually a small depression on the right-hand side of the small entranceway that could hold a small disk. When I asked Mou if there was actually a gold disk, his answer was:

Yes.

When I followed up by inquiring if this was actually how the ancients opened the portal, he went into more detail.

This too is natural manipulation. The gold is used because it is pure. It cannot be made into other things. You need something that cannot be changed. You cannot make lead into gold.

Hayu Marca was an opening where someone could have entered and traveled through time and used a golden disc to open the portal. Residents of the time could only associate such travel as leaving to visit the Gods. Maybe they actually did.

STONEHENGE

Stone construction at Stonehenge, England. Dollarphotoclub.

One of the best known prehistoric monuments in the World is located near Amesbury, England. Stonehenge consists of a series of huge stone structures that are constructed in a symmetry that has astrological implications. As our modern scientists study the structure, they have come to realize that the builders needed to have a sophisticated understanding of mathematics and geometry—not exactly what we thought was being taught during the Bronze Age.

Archeologists say the first phase of work on the site can be dated to 3,000 years before the birth of Christ, early in the Bronze Age. Work continued over hundreds of years with the large inner circle being built around 2500 BC. For a complete history on the site I would refer you to the official website: www. english-heritage.org.uk.

Portion of Stonehenge used to study the stars at Stonehenge. Dollarphotoclub.

Scientists have come to realize that there are many significant astrological features incorporated in the alignments of the stones. This evidence indicates that Stonehenge and other stone rings were used as astrological observatories. The circle is aligned with the summer and winter equinox, as well as the southerly rising and northerly setting of the moon. Stonehenge was clearly used for observation of the heavens as well as for religious rituals.

Another obvious question involves how humans living in the Bronze Age had the ability to erect such a heavy and elaborate stone structure to such a precise alignment. Add to that the fact that the stones were placed with a precision that would test modern techniques. Some of the structure stones are an igneous (fire-formed) rock type that were mined from an area 150 miles away in what is now Wales and would have been transported to the site crossing several major rivers.

Let me add another historical note. Archeologists often assume the stones would have been transported in primitive carts. The first recorded evidence of a wheel and axle took place around 3500 BC, about the same time construction began at Stonehenge. First use of the wheel also took place in faraway Mesopotamia or Iraq—nowhere near England.

I started off by asking the guide the purpose of Stonehenge. He replied:

Ritualistic.

It is generally agreed that rituals were performed at Stonehenge. My next question was if it had anything to do with aliens. His one word answer left little doubt:

Indeed.

What was its purpose?

It was built to connect to humans. Rituals were separate.

I thought it would be interesting to find out a little more about how it helped aliens and human beings to connect, so I asked Mou: Who built Stonehenge? He clarified the purpose of the structure.

We built it to teach the math of the stars for
you to understand what it was all about.

Many different features were added to the stone structure through the centuries. I asked how long it took the aliens to build their part of the structure.

Oh, two years. We had cranes.

Sometimes I do not know if Mou is pulling my leg or not. I might be gullible, but I guess that explains how the large stones were lifted into place. While construction of various ritualistic features took place for almost 1,000 years, according to our alien guide, the intricate core was built in only two years by the aliens. There was still no solid explanation of how the huge stones were transported almost 200 miles crossing three major rivers. Once again his answer did not match any current scientific theories.

UFOs carried them there. There are many missing.
All the smalls were carried away by other people
for building homes many years later.

I asked if aliens still use Stonehenge for any reason. He replied:

No, it was used for about 200 years.

Apparently, the structure was used by humans during many centuries for ritualistic purposes, but the aliens only used it for about 200 years to teach the populace about the heavens. When I questioned a general guide that was not an alien, he had said:

Yes. First alien beings dealt with
circles and triangles. Crop circles.

So aliens are responsible for crop circles?

Yes.

What a perfect lead in for the next part of this chapter!

CROP CIRCLES

The Mowing -Devil:

Or, Strange *NEWS* out of

Hartford - ſhire.

Being a True Relation of a Farmer, who Bargainit with a Poor Mower, about the Cutting down Three Half-Acres of Oats: upon the Mower's asking too much, the F mer ſwore, That the Devil ſhould Mow it, rather than h And ſo it fell out, that that very Night, the Crop of o ſhew'd as if it had been all of a Flame: but next Morni appear'd ſo neatly Mow'd by the Devil, or ſome Infernal tit, that no Mortal Man was able to do the like. Alſo, How the ſaid Oats ly now in the Field, and the Ow was not Power to fetch them away.

Licenſed, April 22th, 1678.

A woodcut engraving from 1678 showing an early crop circle.

Crop circles have been getting the attention of man for a very long time. The earliest recording of a crop circle occurred in 1678, in Hartfordshire, England. An actual woodcut engraving was made of the circle. The locals referred to it as the "mowing devil" since it never occurred to them that it might be the work of extraterrestrials. One night I asked the master guide how long the aliens have been creating crop circles and the answer was:

*For as long as
they have existed.*

(Keep in mind that we confirmed there have been aliens since the beginning of time, so I think it's a logical assumption that a lot of ancient farmers were quite surprised when they checked their fields.) When I asked the purpose of crop circles, the guide said:

Awareness.

Aliens actually want humans to know they are around! There has been a lot of discussion about how the circles are constructed. I asked our alien guide why extraterrestrials create crop circles and he gave a little more detail. His reply was:

Fun and to tell those behind us where we are at.

I followed up by asking if they were some type of map and he answered:

Sure, they tell our plans.

When humans try to fake the circles, they use boards to flatten the crop. I asked the guide how they bent over the wheat and he replied:

A crop circle showing the grass being laid over without breaking. Dollarphotoclub.

Forces of air.

In a later session, I tried to get some more information on the crop circles and how they made them by inquiring if they need a special type of vehicle to trace such intricate details in the fields. His answer reinforced, but also showed another aspect of aliens, their sense of humor.

No, it's air. We love messing with you.

I guess in many ways humans really are easy to mess with. Some investigators thought they might use magnetic force to create the images. When I asked the question, his reply was:

No.

The photograph above shows a crop circle with the blades of wheat being laid over without being broken.

Since the advent of our rapid communication systems, it has been proven that many of the crop circles are hoaxes. Based on my research and information, it is also proven that many of the crop circles are created by an alien presence and therefore would be placed in the unexplainable category by researchers.

Perhaps the best example of an unexplainable crop circle occurred on July 7, 1996, near the famous Stonehenge site. What makes this set of circles so remarkable is that it was made in broad daylight in about forty-five minutes!

On that date, a pilot and photographer were flying around the famous Stonehenge site taking mid-afternoon pictures. The pilot had to re-fuel so he returned to the airport. Approximately forty minutes later, he returned and found what is shown in the image on page 67 in the field next to the famous site. The circles appeared to make a fractal formation called a "julia set" (a complex math equation) and thus the formation got its name: The Julia Set.

While doing research, I ran across the website of Lucy Pringle, http://shop.lucypringle.co.uk. She is a founding member of the Center for Crop Circle Studies and has done extensive lectures and studies of the subject. Lucy managed to

A crop circle forming a mathematical "Julia Set" near Stonehenge, England.
Copyright Lucy Pringle.

interview an individual who observed the creation of the circle. What follows is a paraphrase of the Pringle interview.

The observer and her son's friend were driving past Stonehenge in July 1996 when she saw cars pulled off on the side of the road opposite the famous site. Her curiosity aroused, she pulled to the edge of the road and observed a very strange sight. Her son's friend pointed out that there appeared to be a corn circle forming in the field in front of them.

They observed what looked to be an apparition, similar to an isolated mist over the field of corn. As the crop circle grew larger, the mist seemed to grow larger along with the intricate design.

"There was a mist about two to three feet off the ground and it was sort of spinning around, and, on the ground, a circular shape was appearing, which seemed to get bigger and bigger as simultaneously the mist got bigger and bigger and swirled faster." As the crowd of observers grew, they became aware they were watching the unimaginable. A crop circle was being built before their very eyes! No one realized what they were observing or the reality of the events taking place before them.

The witness observed there was a clear space between the ground and the mist. It was a calm summer's day and there was no wind to blame. When asked how long the event lasted, she stated that she'd lost track of time but believed it was in excess of twenty minutes. She was uncertain as to the color of the mist,

A crop circle from Italy. Dollarphotoclub.

but stated it was not brown, blue, nor pink. The witness was emphatic that the mist was not coming from the ground and did not go far up into the sky.

As you can see from the interview, this is obviously a case where the creation of the crop circle was definitely not a hoax and her description agrees with what our guide told us about how the circles are formed. I would submit that there is no logical explanation of how the circles were formed other than by aliens. As I pointed out earlier in the chapter, aliens do have a longtime affection for Stonehenge.

Crop circles are found in all parts of the world. This image shows one in Poirino, Italy.

I tried to solve the mystery of how the aliens could create intricate crop circles without being seen by people who are nearby.

Most UFOs are from different dimensions.

I think the guide was telling me that aliens operated in a dimension that was not visible to humans at the time the circles were constructed. When I posed the question to the guide, his answer was not exactly clear.

Yes, all is done with smoke and mirrors.

I can't say that answer was a big help. I continued to be bothered by the smoke and mirror explanation, so when we gained the ability to communicate with Mou, I inquired if there were times that motherships could not be seen by humans. His answers were pretty explicit.

We just go stealth. We have shown your scientists the simple form of this. We change an electron force so light goes through us. We are there, you just cannot detect us.

While changing electron force may be pretty common for an alien, it is a hard concept for my human intellect to comprehend. I followed up by stating that he was saying no change of size or shape of the ship was involved with the disappearing act. He replied:

> *Right, we cannot change our mass, just hide it.*
> *Mass is hard to change. It can be done but it takes*
> *too much energy. We cannot hold that much energy*
> *in a ship. So we play with the way we look.*

I hope that explanation sheds a little light on how the crop circles seem to appear from out of nowhere. There is actually an alien ship present, you just cannot see it because of their advanced technology.

SACSAYHUAMAN INCA FORTRESS

A massive fort built with intricate detail near Cusco, Peru. Dollarphotoclub.

A close up of the intricate patter of huge stones at the Cusco fortress. Dollarphotoclub.

Located near the city of Cusco, Peru, there was a massive fort constructed defying logic for the methods of the era. The walls of stone were cut and stacked in such a precise manner that the construction would be next to impossible for modern stone masons.

Constructed without any type of mortar, joints in the wall are so tight, a piece of paper cannot be placed between the stones. Add to that the fact that some of the stones weigh up to 360 tons and were mined as much as thirty-five miles away. The foundation stone is limestone and the outer walls are diorite, a very hard igneous stone type. Inner buildings and towers are made from a third stone type that would have to be quarried thirty-five miles away. Why would they use three diverse stone types for their fortress?

As you look at the detailed picture of the stone construction, a lot of questions come to mind. Why would they use such massive stones or why would they construct the wall like a jigsaw puzzle. It is not like they were trying to defend themselves from modern weapons. Could they have been trying to defend themselves from alien attacks? When I asked why the fort was built, I found out that sometimes the obvious answer is the correct answer.

To keep out another people.

That answer is going to disappoint a lot of people. When I said: "So, the reason for building the fortress had nothing to do with aliens," he stated:

Right.

Not everything constructed by the ancients can be attributed to aliens, and this is one example. When I asked the master guide if the Inca's had help from the aliens in constructing the fortress at Sacasayhuaman his reply was:

Like the pyramids. Some of that and some by man.

How did they lift the rocks into place?

Lower portions came first. Used scaffold.

From the sound of that answer, it seems like the aliens did not help with the physical construction. When I asked Mou if extraterrestrials assisted in the construction of the fortress, he answered in the negative.

We did not nor did we help with the Great Wall.

That answer still left a mystery about how the stone could have been cut to such intricate detail. Mou answered in detail.

*Oh, that we taught them with a simple crystal laser
with sun light through a curved mirror. All children on my
planet made them at play. Quite like a magnifying glass.*

That answered how they could have cut the stones, but the quarry sites were far from the fortress site. How they could have moved the stones over such distances remains a mystery. Our guide's answer filled in the details.

You lack the knowledge of the forgotten ones. You have just begun to use magnet power again. In the old forgotten times people used magnets to move heavy things. In those times they would put a magnet on the ground and one on a heavy thing and move it over the ground. If much material was needed you would make a rail. It made work possible.

Having an engineering background, I found it hard to believe that the early cultures would have magnets strong enough to move such heavy objects. I asked how they moved the really heavy rocks.

More magnets, easy.

Moving those rocks would take an awful lot of magnets, so I asked him if aliens gave the locals the magnets. I think he was starting to lose patience with me from his answer.

You dig them out of the ground.

I guess he could have easily said, "You dig them out of the ground, stupid." Some of the stones used in the construction are huge. Thinking there would be an ulterior motive for using such large blocks, I asked Mou why such large blocks were used. His answer made sense.

Faster to build.

No mysteries solved in that answer! I asked how long it took to build the fort; he replied:

About twenty years your time.

The ancient residents of Peru had access to technology provided by the aliens that allowed them to construct intricate structures. In some instances, such as the Nazca Lines and Palpa flat mountain, the extraterrestrials did all the work, but in other instances the bulk of the construction was carried by the ancient peoples.

Our early cultures around the world constructed many amazing structures that defy our modern imagination. Our spirit guides have given the answers to what really took place during the past millenniums. The best evidence of their help in the past are the incredible structures that still stand as a testament to the aid given to the ancients by the visitors from space.

CHAPTER 5

FAMOUS ALIEN SIGHTINGS

As I conducted my research, I came to realize that a lot of really famous people claimed in public to have witnessed alien flying machines. They come from all walks of life, including famous astronomers, pilots, and even American Presidents!

CLYDE TOMBAUGH

DISCOVERER OF PLUTO SEES UFOS

Perhaps the most qualified person ever to claim to observe a UFO was astronomer **Clyde Tombaugh**, who discovered Pluto in our Solar System in 1930. On August 20, 1949, just three years after the Roswell incident, he stated publicly that he'd observed six to

eight rectangles of light in an arranged formation flying near Las Cruces, New Mexico. He said they were window-like, yellowish-green in color, and moved in a northwest to southeast direction.

He also reported sighting other green fireballs in late 1948 with other sightings that continued through the early 1950s. In 1956, he described his observations as follows:

> I have seen three objects in the last seven years, which defied any explanation of known phenomenon, such as Venus, atmospheric optic, meteors, or planes. I am a highly skilled, professional astronomer. In addition, I have seen three green fireballs which were unusual in behavior from normal green fireballs....I think that several reputable scientists are being unscientific in refusing to entertain the possibility of extraterrestrial origin and nature.[1]

In the 1950s, this type of thinking on the part of such a famous academic was considered quite radical.

GEMINI IV PILOT JAMES MCDIVITT

DESCRIBES SPACECRAFT

United States astronauts are some of the most responsible and highly trained individuals in our armed forces. In June 1965, James McDivitt and Ed White were selected to pilot the Gemini IV space capsule. While orbiting the Earth and passing over Hawaii he witnessed, filmed, and photographed an unknown object. Here is a quote from the Major:

> I was flying with Ed White. He was sleeping at the time, so I don't have anybody to verify my story. We were drifting in space with the control engines shut down and all the instrumentation off [when] suddenly [an object] appeared in the window. It had a very definite shape—a cylindrical object—it was white; it had a long arm that stuck out on the side. I don't know whether it was a very small object up close or a very large object a long ways away. There was nothing to judge by. I really don't know how big it was. We had two cameras that were just floating in the spacecraft at the time, so I grabbed one and took a picture of [the object] and grabbed the other and took a picture. Then I turned on the rocket control systems because I was afraid we might hit it. At the time, we were drifting—without checking I have no idea which way we were going—but as we drifted up a little farther the sun shone on the window of the spacecraft. The windshield was dirty—just like in an automobile, you can't

see through it. So I had the rocket control engines going again and moved the spacecraft so that the window was in darkness again—the object was gone. I called down later and told them what had happened and they went back and checked their records of other space debris that was flying around, but we were never able to identify what it could have been. The film was sent back to NASA and reviewed by some NASA film technicians. One of them selected what he thought was what we talked about, at least before I had a chance to review it. It was not the picture—it was a picture of a sun reflection on the window.[2]

Interestingly enough, the movie and photograph of the incident taken by McDivitt was never released by the government. Upon landing, the film was sent to NASA for analysis. Four days later, they released four pictures of the object, but McDivitt stated that the released pictures were not the cylindrical object he had observed from the Gemini capsule.

FRANK BORMAN AND JAMES LOVELL
HOUSTON WE HAVE A BOGEY

Another incident was reported in December 1965, when Frank Borman and James Lovell saw a strange object during their second orbit of Gemini VII. Mission control told Borman that he was observing their own titan booster rocket, but he confirmed he could see the booster in addition to an entirely different object.

Portions of the transcript (GT 7/6, tape 51, pages 4,5,6) from Gemini 7 are reproduced here.[3] The following conversation took place between the spacecraft and the ground control at Houston and referred to a sighting at the start of the second revolution of the fligh:.

Spacecraft: Gemini Seven here. Houston, how do you read?

Capcom: Loud and clear Seven; go ahead.

Spacecraft: Bogey at 10 o'clock high.

Capcom: This is Houston. Say again, Seven.

Spacecraft: Said we have a bogey at 10 o'clock high.

Capcom: Roger, Gemini 7, is that the booster or is that an actual sighting?

Spacecraft: We have several, looks like debris up here. Actual sighting.

Capcom: You have any more information? Estimate distance and speed?

Spacecraft: We also have the booster in sight.

Capcom: Understand you also have the booster in sight. Roger.

Spacecraft: Yeah, have a very, very many—look like hundreds of little particles banked on the left out about three to four miles.

Capcom: Understand you have many small particles going by on the left. At what distance?

Spacecraft: Oh, about—it looks like a path to the vehicle at ninety degrees.

Capcom: Roger, understand they are about three to four miles away.

Spacecraft: They are passed now—they were in polar orbit.

Capcom: Roger, understand they are about three or four miles away.

Spacecraft: That's what it appeared like. That's roger.

Capcom: Were these particles in addition to the booster and the bogey at 10 o'clock?

Spacecraft: Roger

Spacecraft (Lovell): I have the booster on *my* side; it's a brilliant body in the sun, against a black background with trillions of particles on it.

It is very clear that Lovell believed at the time, and still does, that he was observing an alien craft. During one of our sessions, I asked the guide if Frank Borman and James Lovell actually saw a UFO while on their Gemini 7 mission. His answer verified that they were not seeing things.

They saw a real UFO.

That statement shows that he was definitely not hallucinating.

MAJOR GORDON COOPER

RADAR PICKS UP UFO DURING PROJECT MERCURY

Anyone under fifty years old probably does not remember Project Mercury. The program ran from 1959 through 1963 and had a goal of putting a human into orbit around the earth. Major Gordon Cooper was one of the seven astronauts selected to fly around the earth in a small capsule. Anyone accepted into the program had to be of the highest standards, experienced fighter pilots, and the best the military had to offer. Major Cooper testified before the United Nations about his experience with extraterrestrials. In 1951, while flying an F-86 Saberjet over West Germany he reported seeing saucer-shaped discs:

I believe that these extra-terrestrial vehicles and their crews are visiting this planet from other planets... [Most astronauts were reluctant to discuss UFOs.] I did have occasion in 1951 to have two days of observation of many flights of them, of different sizes, flying in fighter formation, generally from east to west over Europe.[4]

He reported seeing a glowing, greenish object approaching his Mercury capsule in 1963 while orbiting the Earth over Australia. The Perth, Australia, tracking station confirmed the sighting. Our government would not allow the reporters to talk to the astronaut concerning the confirmed sighting. After retiring from the service, Cooper made the following statement:

For many years I have lived with a secret, in a secrecy imposed on all specialists in astronautics. I can now reveal that every day, in the USA, our radar instruments capture objects of form and composition unknown to us. And there are thousands of witness reports and a quantity of documents to prove this, but nobody wants to make them public. Why? Because authority is afraid that people may think of God-knows-what kind of horrible invaders. So the password still is: We have to avoid panic by all means.[5]

Gordon Cooper is correct; the public perception of the nature of aliens is one of the reasons that the information is kept from us by our Governments.

NEIL ARMSTRONG AND EDWIN "BUZZ" ALDRIN

ALIENS ON THE MOON

We have all heard of a man on the moon, but did you know that the first astronauts to walk on the moon recorded a strong alien presence in the form of huge spacecraft parked on the edge of a crater. According to Neil Armstrong, both he and Edwin "Buzz" Aldrin saw alien ships shortly after their landing on the moon in July 1969. Former NASA employee Otto Binder heard one of the astronauts refer to a light in a crater during the television transmission. Mission control requested additional information followed by silence in the transmission. According to the source, the transmission was blocked to the public.

Binder stated that radio hams with their own VHF receiving stations that bypassed the broadcast outlets recorded the following transmissions:

NASA: What's there? Mission Control calling Apollo 11...

Apollo 11: These babies are huge, Sir! Enormous! OH MY GOD! You wouldn't believe it! I'm telling you there are other spacecraft out there, lined up on the far side of the crater edge! They're on the Moon watching us![6]

So much for full disclosure by NASA. Apparently the aliens warned us to stay away from the moon. At a later NASA symposium, Neil Armstrong discussed what happened there with a professor who wishes to remain anonymous.

Professor: What REALLY happened out there with Apollo 11?

Armstrong: It was incredible, of course we had always known there was a possibility; the fact is, we were warned off! (by the Aliens). There was never any question then of a space station or a moon city.

Professor: How do you mean "warned off"?

Armstrong: I can't go into details, except to say that their ships were far superior to ours, both in size and technology—boy, were they big! And menacing! No, there is no question of a space station.

Professor: But NASA had other missions after Apollo 11?

Armstrong: Naturally; NASA was committed at that time, and couldn't risk panic on Earth. But it really was a quick scoop and back again.[7]

I asked Mou to verify if Armstrong and Aldrin really saw a UFO during the Apollo 11 flight. He supported their statements:

They first saw lights and then a hover craft.

That statement verified that they actually saw a UFO, but when I asked if we were warned not to come back to the moon, his answer did not back up the statements of Neil Armstrong.

No, there was never contact. They were welcome.
It is a good thing you want to know more. In fact, your people
have learned many things that we use in our sciences.

In one of our sessions with Mou, I inquired if aliens really have a base on the moon. His reply was:

No. We moved out when you came, but the Astro
belt and Mars, Jupiter, and I think Saturn.

As part of the effort of NASA to keep the sightings of UFOs from the public, the code name "Santa Claus" was used to indicate their presence. When James Lovell on Apollo 8 came around from the backside of the moon, he made the statement: "Please be informed that there is a Santa Claus."[8] The clear inference for NASA was that he had spotted alien craft on the backside of the moon. During one of our sessions, I asked Mou to confirm if they encountered aliens while on the back side of the moon and if their code name was Santa Claus. His answer was short and to the point.

Yes.

Many theorists expound that the moon is hollow. I thought this would be an appropriate time, so I asked our alien guide about this. His reply indicated that Santa Claus's workshop might have a back-door entrance on the back side of the moon.

Yes. The dark side is its entrance.

Not only does the moon seem to be hollow, but there is an entrance on the backside where nosey earthlings can't see their coming and goings. According to the various websites, there are more statements by our astronauts concerning encounters with unidentified flying objects. As you can see, the vivid descriptions quoted leave little doubt that the individuals were quite definitive in their descriptions of events.

While we were on the subject of the hollow moon, I asked if there were any other hollow planets. His answer caught me by surprise.

Two.

When I asked which two, he replied:

Uranus and Neptune. Some of the back planet moons have had activity. Some planets are solid. Some are as thin as an egg shell and most are in between. The thicker the surface, the more likely life. Solid planets are not good either. You have no pushing and pulling so you have mountains and such.

Assuming his statements are true, our astronomers have a lot of learning to do. It seems as though NASA might know an awful lot more about our Solar System than has been released to the people.

JIMMY CARTER AND RONALD REAGAN
WOULD YOU BELIEVE PRESIDENTS OF THE UNITED STATES?

On January 22, 1969, two years before he became governor, Jimmy Carter was attending a Lion's Club meeting in Leary, Georgia. At about 7:15 p.m., a red and green glowing orb moved rapidly across the southwestern Georgia sky. In a 2005 interview, Carter made the following statement about the event:

All of a sudden, one of the men looked up and said, "Look, over in the west!" And there was a bright light in the sky. We all saw it. And then the light, it got closer and closer to us. And then it stopped; I don't know how far away, but it stopped beyond the pine trees. And all of a sudden, it changed color to blue, and then it changed to red, then back to white. And we were trying to figure out what in the world it could be, and then it receded into the distance.[9]

At a Southern Governors' Conference, he made the statement:

I don't laugh at people any more when they say they've seen UFOs; I've seen one myself.[10]

In the interest of political equality, one of our most famous Republican presidents, Ronald Reagan, also told of having an incident with a UFO. While flying in a Cessna Citation aircraft in 1974, during the time he was governor of California, his plane was followed by a strange light. There were four people on board: the pilot, Bill Paynter, two security guards, and the governor. The most detailed description of the incident was given by the pilot (www.mysterousuniverse. org/2014/01/the-gipper-ufo/).

It appeared to be several hundred yards away. It was a fairly steady light until it began to accelerate. Then it appeared to elongate. Then the light took off. It went up at a 45-degree angle at a high rate of speed. Everyone on the plane was surprised. The UFO went from a normal cruise speed to a fantastic speed instantly. If you give an airplane power, it will accelerate—but not like a hot rod, and that's what this was like.[11]

A week after the event, Reagan was doing an interview with Norman C. Miller, bureau chief for the *Wall Street Journal*. During the interview, the future president made the statement:

We followed it for several minutes. It was a bright white light. We followed it to Bakersfield, and all of a sudden to our utter amazement it went straight up into the heavens.[12]

It is not generally known, but as president, Ronald Reagan worried about an alien invasion. He even voiced this worry in 1987 when he spoke before the General Assembly of the United Nations. Here is an excerpt from that speech:

In our obsession with antagonisms of the moment, we often forget how much unites all the members of humanity. Perhaps we need some outside, universal threat to make us recognize this common bond. I occasionally think, how quickly our differences worldwide would vanish if we were facing an alien threat from outside this world. And yet, I ask, is not an alien force already among us?[13]

That is pretty amazing stuff coming from two very different presidents of the United States. It certainly makes you wonder about what they know and we don't.

SAUCERS OVER WASHINGTON, DC

During the 1950s, UFOs took an active interest in flying over our Nation's Capital. From July 12 to July 29, 1952, unidentified objects were recorded on the radars of Andrews Air Force Base and what is now Reagan International Airport. What makes these sightings unusual is that during the two-week period, they were observed by thousands of people, many of them from the military. Radar operators even witnessed the objects on their screens and visually as well. During the event, they flew over the White House, Pentagon, and Capitol Building. So much for an iron clad defense during the beginning of the Cold War.

In one well-documented incident, Capital Airlines pilot S.C. Pierman was waiting to be cleared for takeoff in his DC-4 when he spotted what he believed to be a meteor. When he checked with the tower, he was told that the objects were visible to the controllers and were closing on his position. The pilot described the objects as "white, tailless, fast-moving lights." He was not the only professional to spot the objects.

Air Force F-94 night fighters were dispatched on several occasions, but were unable to chase down the objects as they seemed to play cat and mouse with the planes. On one occasion, a fighter plane was actually surrounded by the objects. The speed of the objects was tracked on radar from 100 mph to 7,200 mph. That is thirteen times the speed of sound, something unobtainable by modern fighter planes. The F-94s that were dispatched were capable of a top speed of 600 mph. No wonder the pilots were frustrated when they tried to close on the UFOs.

This time the government outdid themselves in coming up with an explanation of what was observed by all the individuals. They blamed it on a temperature inversion! I guess it never dawned on them that temperature inversions in the DC area don't last for two weeks. In spite of the official explanation, I asked Mou if the objects seen over the Capital building in 1952 were alien ships. His answer:

Yes.

When I inquired as to why the ships were there for such an extended period of time, he replied:

Ha Ha Ha. Rides. President wanted a ride.

He just stated that our president at the time, Harry Truman, wanted to take a ride on a UFO and he thought it was funny! I definitely needed to clarify that statement so I said, "Are you saying the president went for a ride in a UFO?"

Yes, three times.

It must have been quite an experience if he went for a ride in a mothership three times. Next, I inquired what the aliens looked like that were taking our President for a ride. He replied:

The little guys with big eyes.

Having no idea who the little guys with big eyes were, I asked if they were the Grays.

No. No one trusts the Grays.

So, the little guys with big eyes took our president, Harry Truman, for three rides on a flying saucer. I wonder if the Secret Service went along? At the beginning of this book I told you there would be events that would stretch your imagination and this is certainly one of them. What has been referred to as Invasion Washington was really our president wanting to go for a ride in a UFO.

Through the years, especially since our space program, very reputable individuals have reported the sightings of UFOs. Our alien guide has verified that most of the famous sightings, often dismissed by our government, were actually observations of our visitors from outer space.

CHAPTER 6

PROJECT BLUE BOOK

I n spite of all the disinformation presented by the United States Air Force, they actually investigated reports of UFOs under a program known as Project Blue Book. The program ran from 1947 until December 1969. It is probably not an accident that the beginning of the project coincided with the incident at Roswell, New Mexico. Details of the program are now made available under the Freedom of Information Act and can be read online. A few of the incidents are quite interesting. I will describe the events that took place from the official reports and then tell what really happened as detailed in our channeling sessions with the spirit of an actual visitor from outer space.

Under this program, investigators classified reports under three categories, CP (which stood for crack pot), Insufficient Data for Evaluation, and Unknown. Unknown stood for reports that could not be discredited. During the period in which Project Blue Book was active, they investigated 12,618 incidents with 701 incidents

categorized as unknown. That means that as hard as the investigators tried, over 700 or approximately 32 reported occurrences a year could not be discredited. There is no way of knowing how many incidents were intentionally labeled in a wrong category. (Also keep in mind that this was before the age of the Internet and mass communication. One can only imagine how many incidents occurred, but were not reported.)

AN UNREFUTED INCIDENT

On July 24, 1952, two Air Force colonels assigned to the Pentagon, each having over 2,000 hours of flying time and the highest security clearances, were flying a B-25 from Hamilton Air Force Base in California to Colorado Springs, Colorado. Around 3:40 p.m., they were over Nevada when they spotted what looked like three F-86s flying in a tight formation.

When the B-25 approached what they thought was our military aircraft, the colonels realized that the vehicles were not F-86s, but three bright silver, delta-winged ships with no tails and or pilot canopies. This was not a design familiar to the officers. The delta-shaped ships made a left bank and passed the two colonels at a distance of 400 to 800 yards, close enough to allow them definitive visual identification. The ships were flying at an extremely high rate of speed estimated to be three times faster than our best fighter aircraft of the period. Whatever they were observing, the vehicles were not related to our military.

When the two officers landed at Colorado Springs, they filed a UFO report with Air Defense Command Headquarters. Flight Service was responsible for keeping track of what aircraft were in the area. Though contacted, they had no record of any military flight in the vicinity of the sightings. Our military did have delta-winged aircraft, but none were within 2,000 miles of the incident and none could come close to the performance of the UFOs. The Pentagon assignments of the individuals involved qualified them to recognize any type of aircraft flying anywhere in the world. There was no way the military could discredit the testimony of the individuals who witnessed the incident. There was no official explanation for what took place in the sky over Nevada on that afternoon. The event was officially classified as "unknown." I figured the event would not be unknown to our alien guide and I was correct. When I asked him if the delta-winged air crafts were UFOs his reply was:

Yes, they witnessed UFOs.

According to Mou, they were definitely correct in classifying this event as "unknown."

DOGFIGHT WITH A UFO

This occurrence shows that aliens can be in what appears to be a very bad humor. On October 1, 1948, an incident happened in which a UFO and a North Dakota National Guard F-51 aircraft got into a type of dogfight. A twenty-five-year old second lieutenant, George F. Gorman, was returning from a cross-country flight. As he was preparing to land, he observed what was thought to be the taillight of another aircraft on his right side.

When he called the tower to report it, he was told the only other aircraft in the area was a Cub at a lower attitude. Gorman had visual contact with the other plane, but still saw the closer light. He decided to investigate the light, so he flew toward it and got within approximately 1,000 yards. He could tell the light was six to eight inches in diameter, but could not determine any body shape of another aircraft. He could see the light was blinking on and off.

As the object grew nearer, the light stopped blinking, made a sharp left turn and buzzed by the tower with the F-51 in pursuit. The light accelerated to 7,000 feet with Gorman chasing. When the light made another turn, the pilot realized he had a problem; he was now on a collision course with the mystery light! Gorman put the plane into a dive to avoid getting rammed by the UFO, narrowly missing it by only several feet. When he pulled out of the dive and turned, he had another rude surprise. The object was once again taking dead aim at the plane and they were once more on a collision course. Gorman had to dive again to avoid being hit by the light.

After the second apparent attempt to ram the airplane, the UFO tired of the "game," accelerated into a climb, and disappeared. His story was partially corroborated by the pilot and passenger in the Cub and two CAA employees who saw the light move over the ground. When he landed, Gorman filed a written report in which he told investigators: "I had the distinct impression that its maneuvers were controlled by thought or reason." Investigators were never able to find any facts to shoot down (pardon the pun) what happened that evening.

This was the official version of what took place based on interviews with the pilot. During one of our sessions with Mou, I asked specifically if Gorman got into a dogfight with a UFO and if the UFO had tried to collide with his plane. His answer was quite enlightening.

> *That was a young pilot. The pilot got into trouble*
> *for that stunt. In no time was he in danger. But the two*
> *crafts came very close. Our crafts have powers so space*
> *junk will not hit us. The craft cannot hit things.*

It seem as though the pilot mistook evasive action by the alien ship as an attempt to collide with his fighter. I find it quite comforting to know that there is little danger in colliding with UFOs. If they can miss space junk, they should be able to avoid our relatively slow-flying aircraft.

A DEADLY ENCOUNTER

Captain Thomas Mantell Jr. was a highly decorated and experienced pilot in the United States Air Force. Awarded the Distinguished Flying Cross for his participation in the Normandy invasion, he logged 2,167 hours in the air. After the war, he was assigned to the 165th Fighter Squadron of the Kentucky Air National Guard where he flew P-51 Mustangs. This was not a man that did stupid things in an airplane!

On January 7, 1948, the Kentucky Highway Patrol received several reports of a large circular object moving in a westbound direction. About 1:45 in the afternoon, the object was sighted from the control tower at Fort Knox. It was described as "very white about one fourth the size of the full moon." The base commander stated that it appeared to have a red border at the bottom. Observers in Ohio also described it:

As having the appearance of a flaming red cone trailing a gaseous green mist. An observer at Lockbourne Army Air Field stated:

Just before leaving it came to very near the ground, staying down for about ten seconds, then climbed at a very fast rate back to its original altitude, 10,000 feet, leveling off and disappearing into the overcast heading 120 degrees. Its speed was greater than 500 mph in level flight.

Captain Mantell was flying one of four P-51 Mustangs that were told to approach the strange object that was climbing in altitude. Some say that Mantell described the object to the tower as: "It looks metallic and of tremendous size." Three of the fighters followed the object in steep pursuit. Mantell did not have oxygen in his aircraft, but continued to climb past 22,500, the elevation at which two of the planes leveled off and ended the pursuit. They reported they saw the object, but described it as so small they could not identify it. He continued the pursuit without oxygen.

According to the air force, the Captain blacked out at 25,000 feet and spiraled out of control, crashing near the Kentucky-Tennessee line. A basic part of pilot training is that you do not go over 15,000 feet without oxygen. An obvious question to be answered is why such a highly experienced pilot would exceed the limits of breathable oxygen until he blacked out. When the body was recovered, his watch read 3:18, the time of the crash. The object was observed until 3:50 by individuals at Godman Field. In this instance, Project Blue Book concluded that Mantell died pursuing a top-secret weather balloon. Another twist to the incident is that Mantell was killed in the crash only a couple of miles from the Hospital in which he was born.

When I asked Mou about this incident, his answer indicated that aliens harbor emotion when humans do stupid things and get themselves in serious trouble. He replied:

No, it was pilot error. It made us sad.
His craft was not made to hold the G's.

The Captain died trying to match the performance of an extraterrestrial vehicle, not chasing a weather balloon.

ANOTHER CLOSE CALL

On July 24, 1948, a DC-3 owned by Eastern Airlines took off on a flight from Houston, Texas, to Atlanta, Georgia. When it was about twenty miles southwest of Montgomery, Alabama, the pilot told the copilot he saw a light dead ahead and closing fast. First thinking it was a jet plane, the crew rapidly came to the conclusion that it was closing much too fast. Fearing a head-on collision, the pilot threw the plane into a tight left turn. As a result, the UFO passed within about 700 feet to the right of the DC-3. The pilot observed that after passing, the object pulled up into a steep climb.

Both of the crew members had a good look at the UFO as it buzzed their plane. It was described as having a B-29-type fuselage with an underside having a deep blue glow. Amazingly, they reported the vehicle having two rows of windows from which bright lights glowed. In addition, a bright trail of orange red flame shot out the back. This was the first time credible individuals gave such a detailed description. A single passenger viewed the object from a window, but he simply described it as a strange eerie streak of light that was very intense.

What makes this incident so interesting is that the UFO was seen by multiple reputable individuals in different locations. A crew chief at Robins Air Force base in Macon, Georgia, also reported seeing a strange vehicle. He described it as being an extremely bright light that passed overhead at a very high rate of speed. In addition, a pilot near the North Carolina-Virginia line reported seeing a bright shooting star in the direction of Montgomery at the same time the DC-3 was maneuvering to avoid being hit by the object. When investigators plotted the reports, they corroborated what would have been the flight path of the UFO. Apparently, this was the first recorded time that competent individuals got a good look at an alien vehicle and lived to tell about it. When I asked Mou if indeed they saw a mothership loaded with aliens, he answered in the affirmative:

Yes, they saw a mothership. At no time were
they in danger of colliding with the ship.

In this chapter I attempt to point out that the government of the United States was actively investigating alien occurrences. In spite of their denials, there were over 700 incidents in that twenty-two-year period that could not be discredited. One evening we were channeling and I asked if I would be safe in printing some of this information. In response to the question, the guide answered with a question:

Do you think you can trust your government?

For twenty-two years, our government studied alien occurrences and could not discredit hundreds of the events. Through different presidents and control of Congress by both parties, these events were kept from the people. Unfortunately, you can trust your government to take extreme measures to keep the truth of aliens from the public.

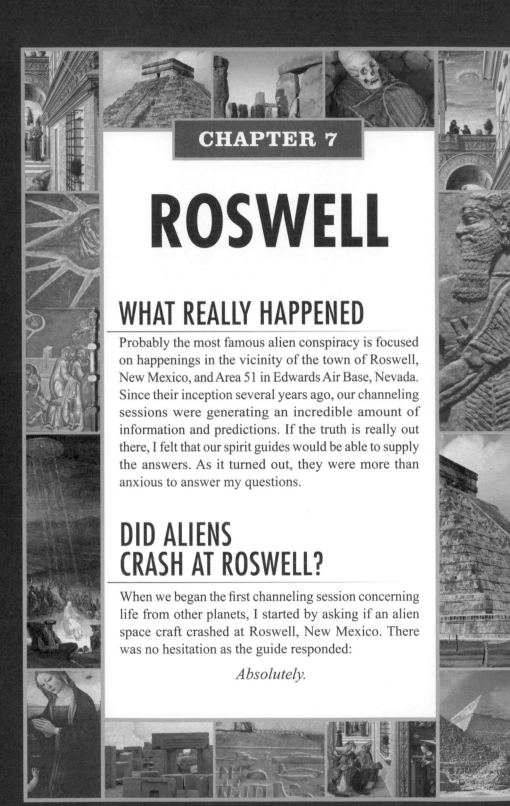

CHAPTER 7

ROSWELL

WHAT REALLY HAPPENED

Probably the most famous alien conspiracy is focused on happenings in the vicinity of the town of Roswell, New Mexico, and Area 51 in Edwards Air Base, Nevada. Since their inception several years ago, our channeling sessions were generating an incredible amount of information and predictions. If the truth is really out there, I felt that our spirit guides would be able to supply the answers. As it turned out, they were more than anxious to answer my questions.

DID ALIENS CRASH AT ROSWELL?

When we began the first channeling session concerning life from other planets, I started by asking if an alien space craft crashed at Roswell, New Mexico. There was no hesitation as the guide responded:

Absolutely.

Not much doubt in that answer! My follow up inquired whether there were aliens killed in the crash, to which the guide said:

Yes.

It was starting to look like the conspiracy theorists might have something to talk about. When I inquired how many aliens were killed in the crash, the answer was:

4 to 6.

Perhaps the best insight into how many aliens were killed in the Roswell crash comes in *The Day After Roswell* by Colonel Philip Corso. Written by the Army officer who had access to the crash debris and secret government files concerning Roswell, the book gives excellent insight into to the role of government. Col. Corso refers to the remains of five aliens being removed from the crash site for future study. This number verifies the estimate of aliens killed told to us by the guide.

According to our guide, it looks like the conspiracy theories surrounding the Roswell incident are based in fact. In this chapter I will attempt to pass on the information as given to me through these sessions. Let me start by telling the historical version of the happenings that would create numerous books, movies, and conspiracy theories.

HISTORY OF ROSWELL

Sometime prior to July 7, 1947, an event took place when an object fell from the sky near Roswell, New Mexico, that would alter our thinking about extraterrestrials forever. The official story by the government is that an experimental weather balloon crashed and the remains of the balloon, as well as the story presented by the Army at the press conference, are proof of what really happened. Conspiracy theorists believe that the government covered up the crash of an alien vehicle. In order to better understand the detailed messages of the heavenly guides concerning the occurrence at Roswell, I will discuss the events that are undisputed.

At the time of the incident, the United States was entering the first throes of the Cold War with the Soviet Union. A lot of secret operations were taking place in the New Mexico desert. Early in July of 1947, our radar operations were showing an increase in unidentified activities over some of our most secret facilities. The United States military feared that the Soviets had developed a secret flying technology that allowed them to violate our air space. Our aircraft was incapable of chasing the mysterious objects that moved rapidly across the radar screens and seemed to change direction on a dime. Our military was very much on edge at the thought that our enemy had the ability to intrude on our air space at will. Many reputable residents of the area reported seeing strange flying objects during this time period.

The city of Roswell, New Mexico, is located in the relatively unpopulated southeastern corner of the state. Not incorporated until 1891, the lack of water and harsh conditions of the area limited development and created an environment basically dedicated to ranching. The rural nature of the area did not go unnoticed by our government, as they established the White Sands Missile Testing Facility and other secretive sites in the vicinity of the town. Much of our early nuclear testing and development took place in this general location.

STRANGE DEBRIS DISCOVERED

On June 14, 1947, a large working ranch, the Foster Homestead, was located about seventy-five miles northwest of the town of Roswell. William Brazel, a foreman on the ranch, found a strange debris field while checking fences. On July 4, he and his wife, son, and daughter rode back to the debris field and collected several pieces of the wreck. According to reports, during the next couple of days, Brazel heard reports that strange flying discs were seen in the area. He took the collected debris to town and told the sheriff that he might have found the debris from one of the reported flying discs. He could have reported the debris to the sheriff as early as July 6. His comments concerning the debris included observations that the materials seemed to have strength characteristics not of this world.

The incident was then reported to the Roswell Army Air Field (RAAF) and Brazel escorted a plain-clothed representative of the Army, Major Jesse Marcel, to the crash site. The major was the first military person to inspect the debris field. He collected several boxes of what he and Brazel found and took it to his commanding officer at the Roswell Army Air Field.

Upon the report of Major Marcel, the military dispatched men and equipment to secure the area and recover the reported remains of the ship. Armed military police maintained site security and civilians were kept from viewing the site. Material was placed in cartons and large portions of the ship were loaded onto trucks and taken to the Roswell Air Field. This process took several days.

THE MILITARY TELLS THE TRUTH, ALMOST

Early on Tuesday, July 8, the Roswell Army Air Field issued the following press release.

The *Roswell Daily Record* tells of a flying saucer crashing in New Mexico. Public Domain.

The many rumors regarding the flying disc became a reality yesterday when the intelligence office of the 509th Bomb group of the Eighth Air Force, Roswell Army Air Field, was fortunate enough to gain possession of a disc through the cooperation of one of the local ranchers and the sheriff's office of Chaves County. The flying object landed on a ranch near Roswell sometime last week. Not having phone facilities, the rancher stored the disc until such time as he was able to contact the sheriff's office, who in turn notified Maj. Jesse A. Marcel of the 509th Bomb Group Intelligence Office. Action was immediately taken and the disc was picked up at the rancher's home. It was inspected at the Roswell Army Air Field and subsequently loaned by Major Marcel to higher headquarters.

The press release was picked up by various news agencies and, on July 8, 1947, the headline of the *Roswell Daily Record* stated: "RAAF Captures Flying Saucer On Ranch in Roswell Region." Anyone interested in the details of this article can find it easily on the Internet. The story was also run in several major newspapers such as the *Sacramento Bee*.

Now here is where the idea of a conspiracy starts to gain momentum. The debris collected at the crash site was sent to the commanding general of the Eighth Air Force, Roger Ramey.

HERE COMES THE GOVERNMENT SPIN

By late in the day on July 8, the general issued a statement that the debris was in fact the remnants of a weather balloon that was recovered by the Roswell Army Air Field personnel. A press conference was held that featured debris that seemed to confirm that the items were actually from a high-altitude balloon. Major Marcel was photographed holding the remains of what seemed to be a balloon and the image was released to the press. The look on the face of Major Marcel in the photograph says it all.

Major Marcel hold sections of a weather balloon for the press at Roswell. Public Domain.

William Brazel, the rancher that found the debris, was detained by the military for interviews at the air base for almost a week. After enjoying the Army hospitality, Brazel stated that the debris was probably the weather balloon, in contrast to his original story. Years later, his children reported that they were threatened to never tell anyone what they had seen.

In an interview many years later, Major Marcel stated that the debris field spread out in a triangular shape, ¾ of a mile long and 200 to 300 feet wide. As you can see, the wreckage of a weather balloon would never cover that much real estate. At the time of the crash, the Major was ordered not to discuss the event and to agree with the official Army statement.

The entire event disappeared from sight for almost thirty years as the public accepted the weather balloon story. Stanton T. Friedman, a ufologist and physicist, obtained an interview with Major Jesse Marcel in 1978. In this interview, Marcel expressed the belief that the crash was indeed an alien aircraft and the military had covered up the event. Needless to say, the conspiracy theories took off like an alien spacecraft after this interview.

PARTICIPANTS SPEAK OUT

Major Marcel passed away in 1986, but his son, Jesse Marcel Jr., published a book in 2009 entitled *The Roswell Legacy*. In this book he describes his firsthand inspection of the debris that was collected by his father before it was shipped to General Ramey. He describes an indestructible type of foil, small I-beams with strange symbols and straw-like pieces that seem to have been optical fiber. None of these materials were used in weather balloons of the period and all of them were never seen in public again.

Colonel Coroso describes inspecting the same type of materials many years later in the Pentagon. The straw-like filaments described by Jesse Marcel did indeed turn out to be fiber-optic filaments. Our scientists reverse engineered the technology from the Roswell crash to create the fiber optics used today. Foil-like material from the site is described exactly alike in both books. A wealth of technological advances have come from the analysis of the debris from the alien craft.

There have been multiple books published concerning the Roswell event that both prove and disprove a government cover up of the crash of an extraterrestrial space craft. The fog of time has clouded any attempt to truly get to the bottom of the Roswell event. Our government has resisted any attempt to release documents concerning the events that took place during June of 1947.

The conspiracy theory concerning the event was revived in 1992 when a book, *Crash at Corona*, written by Stanton T. Friedman and Don Berliner, detailed a cover up of a UFO recovery based on anonymous documents dropped off at a UFO researcher's house in 1984 by a government whistle blower. These documents were supposedly copies of the 1952 briefing notes for the incoming president, Dwight Eisenhower. Apparently, the new president was told of a high-level government agency whose purpose was to investigate alien remains recovered at Roswell and keep the findings hidden from the public. If the new President Eisenhower was to be informed, it is probably a safe assumption that the president at the time, Harry Truman, was well aware of the Roswell events.

REST EASY, OUR GOVERNMENT REPORTS

During the 1980s, as a result of several books being published and interviews with participants, public interest continued to grow concerning the Roswell event.

Congress requested that the General Accounting Office review the facts concerning the incident. As a result, the GAO produced a nearly 1,000-page report in 1994 entitled "The Roswell Report: Fact Versus Fiction in the New Mexico Desert." It blamed the incident on debris from a secret military program named Project Mogul. This project consisted of a special type of high altitude spy balloon.

In 1997, the Government published another report entitled "Roswell Report: Case Closed." This report further elaborated on Project Mogul and reported that the "alien body sightings" were actually dummies dropped from high altitude test balloons in the 1950s. Unfortunately, the real dummies doing the report did not realize the crash took place in 1947, not the 1950s. In addition, when research teams looked into the track taken by the Project Mogul balloons, the paths did not come near the actual crash site. No wonder the conspiracy theories thrived!

OUR GUIDES SPEAK THE TRUTH

Before one of our sessions, I made up a list of detailed questions concerning the events around Roswell. I began by asking if our government has proof of the presence of extraterrestrials and the answer was an unequivocal:

Yes, positively do.

My next question asked if a conspiracy existed and did the government keep it a secret from the public and his reply was, as I expected,

Yes

I could not help but ask why they wanted to keep it a secret. His answer was not a surprise:

Government control.

That answer hit a nerve in light of the current scandal at NSA, our super-secret spy agency, now capable of recording our emails and phone calls! I read that the government had actually been able to question surviving extraterrestrials, so I asked if any of the aliens survived. The answer was:

No.

Quoting Col. Corso's book, apparently a very interesting situation occurred when the military police took over the security at the crash site. One of the aliens survived the crash, badly injured, and attempted to escape the area. While trying to crawl up the side of an arroyo, the MPs shot and killed the lone survivor. The bodies were placed in specially constructed coffins and preserved in some type of blue liquid.

It appears that the conspiracy theory stating that one of the beings lived was partially correct. Unfortunately, the military ended the life of the survivor. Next, I asked about the size of the alien craft that crashed:

Not as large as others.

He kind of ducked that question, so I attempted to get more detail. I asked if he had any idea how many feet the ship was in diameter. He replied:

I would not know that.

Since our guide for the evening was not an alien spirit, he can be excused for not knowing the size of the ship. Apparently, the size of the crashed ship would remain a mystery to us on this evening, but I did get the impression that there were some really big ones out there. A description of the craft occurs in *The Day After Roswell*. The book states: "It was small, but looked more like the flying wing shape of an old Curtis than an ellipse or a saucer. And it had two tail fins on the top sides of the delta's feet that pointed up and out." It was basically intact, but had a large slit in the side.

My next question asked if the government had the remains and the answer was once again:

Yes.

When asked where the government kept the remains the reply was:

Airbase.

I asked if the airbase was near Roswell and the answer was:

Yes, and 51.

AREA 51

Another area associated with UFO conspiracy theories is referred to as Area 51. Located in the southern portion of Nevada, eighty-three miles north-northwest of Las Vegas, there is a remote detachment of Edwards Air Force Base known as Groom Lake. On the southern shore of the lake, there is a large, super-secret military airfield whose official primary purpose is listed as undetermined. It is believed that the U-2 spy plane of Cold War fame was developed here. In spite of the secrecy surrounding the area, the general consensus of opinion is that the airfield supports development of secret weapons and experimental systems. Area 51's high-security status would make it a perfect place to store extraterrestrial bodies or apparatus.

In 2013, the government finally admitted to the existence of Area 51 in documents obtained through the Freedom of Information Act by George Washington University's National Security Archive. The documents verified how the Nevada site was the home of the U-2 spy plane project and was utilized for decades for secret activities. One subject, conspicuous by its absence, is the mention of aliens.

Getting back to our sessions, the guide certainly seemed to be well acquainted with all of the aspects of the talking points of a government conspiracy theory. Next, I asked what was so special about Area 51. His response was:

Experimental test facility with clues and evidence from UFO.

It is a fact that access to Area 51 is highly restricted and top secret. It was becoming more evident that our guides have little respect for government secrecy.

ALIEN AUTOPSIES

There are many pictures out there showing details of alleged alien autopsies. When I asked if autopsies were performed on the extraterrestrials killed in the crash, he replied:

Yes.

My next question was what did the autopsies reveal? To that question, the guide responded:

Basically that they are not human and study of the brain was most concern. They are highly intelligent beings.

Do any real photographs of aliens exist? His answer to this was:

Yes.

But when asked if they were made public, the answer was:

No.

So much for putting any faith in the pictures on the Internet! When I asked if the photos would ever become public, his answer was:

Perhaps in time.

At least there is hope that we might see what an extraterrestrial actually looks like some day.

WHEN IN DOUBT, ASK AN ALIEN SPIRIT

Since I don't expect to live long enough to see actual pictures of the Roswell aliens released by the government, I thought I would ask our alien guide to describe the appearance of the aliens killed in the Roswell crash.

Taller than the Little Whites, Shorter than the Grays, long arms and bubble heads and big eyes. No noses and a big mouth.

Mou took it for granted that we knew how tall the Little Whites and Grays stood, but I will let that slide for the time being. With long arms and a bubble head with big eyes they would definitely stand out in a crowd.

The heart of all good conspiracy theories is the government getting involved and manipulating the information given to the public to keep the truth from the citizens. At the time of the incident, the rancher, William Brazel, changed his story after being the guest of the military for a week. I inquired if the government forced the rancher to change his story and the answer was:

Yes.

When asked if the military substituted the wreckage of a weather balloon for the debris from the ship, the reply was also:

Yes.

The conspiracy theory seems to be a little less of a theory and more a reality!

PRESIDENTIAL AWARENESS

I asked if our government has made direct contact with the aliens. Our guide's next reply was:

Some have, yes. Your President Eisenhower was one.

That answer caught me off guard and I repeated myself by asking if the guide was saying President Eisenhower made direct contact with aliens. His message in reply was:

He and your President Truman were aware.

When I asked what role President Truman played, the answer was:

He saw the remains.

It seems like President Truman was deeply involved in the decision to keep the events from the American public. It seems a little unfair, since we learned in an earlier chapter that he actually took rides on a flying saucer. In my opinion, the decision to cover up the alien information must have been made at the highest or presidential level.

In 1947, the year of the Roswell incident, then President Truman appointed James Forrestal as Secretary of Defense. Independently wealthy, he was known as being extremely dedicated and an excellent administrator. As the head of the military, he and the president would have been the individuals in government to make the final decisions about how to handle the proof of extraterrestrials. It is safe to assume that he would have been involved in any conspiracy, if one exists.

SECRECY ENFORCED

Suddenly, on March 29, 1949, Secretary Forrestall was abruptly removed from office. By April 2, he was committed, against his wishes, to the 16th floor of the Bethesda Naval Hospital for some kind of a breakdown. It is an interesting question why he was committed to a military facility when he was no longer a member of the military, having been removed from office days before he was forcibly confined to the hospital.

On May 22, 1949, James Forrestall allegedly committed suicide by jumping out of a window at the Bethesda Naval Hospital. He was supposedly being treated for emotional exhaustion, paranoia, and suicidal tendencies. He remains the highest ranking American official to have ever committed suicide. I think you can probably see where I am headed with this one.

I asked the master guide if James Forrestal was involved with the Roswell cover up. His answer was:

Yes.

My next question went right to the heart of the matter: Was Forestall killed because of his knowledge of UFO's? His answer was:

*He planned to speak and reveal. Could
not live with the decision to keep the truth hidden.*

Did he commit suicide?

He had two choices.

Sounds like the Men in Black gave him an offer he couldn't refuse! My belief is that either choice would have had the same result. The next question asked who was responsible for his death. The answer was:

The government unseen.

It started to look like there was a conspiracy within a cover up. Earlier, I'd asked the guide if the government had ever executed anyone for their knowledge of UFOs and his answer had been:

Execute, no.

My guess is he did not consider pushing someone out or forcing him to jump from a window an execution.

A SHOCKING REVELATION

Harry Truman was president during the Roswell incident but Dwight Eisenhower became president in 1953, four-and-one-half years after the Roswell event. I inquired as to Eisenhower's involvement with the cover up. The guide's reply almost surprised me out of my chair. He said:

*I would say your president concerned himself
with aliens and with the idea of travel through time. He
believed that aliens came from a future time. He was correct.*

We were just informed that aliens are time travelers from a future time! After catching my breath, I said "are you telling me aliens are from a future time?" His reply was:

*Yes, space and time exists within the
stratosphere but not so in the realms.*

We had been told in earlier sessions that there was no time in the realms. My follow up was: Are aliens humans from a future time?

They are not human per se. They are a different species of life.

Is there such a thing as an alien portal? The guide replied:

*They, like souls and time travelers,
enter and exit through portals.*

There is an awful lot of information in those last two statements! The guide was saying that souls have the ability to time travel and exit and enter through portals. Aliens use these same portals to travel back to the future and return to our present time. This must be how souls can tell of the future and past.

My next question inquired if there was direct contact after Roswell? The pointer on the spirit board spelled out:

*Yes, after Roswell brought about
visits to exchange information.*

DIRECT PRESIDENTIAL CONTACT

Are you saying our government made direct contact with the extraterrestrials?

Some have, yes. Your President Eisenhower was one.

Not only did our government make contact with the aliens, it appears they were having regular conversations! I was curious about what they discussed, so I asked if the aliens wanted their stuff back. The answer was:

Yes.

We certainly had a bunch of debris from the crash site at Roswell. Did we give it back?

Not all. Some was given in exchange for information.

Next I inquired what else the government wanted to know from them. He replied:

They have been a source of study for their ability to clone. Research records were found at the Roswell site.

Are you saying the aliens have been trying to clone humans?

They were working on that.

Did they accomplish their cloning project?

Not fully. Scientists on earth have for years been studying the knowledge found out at Roswell. Your government controls the records.

So much for the Freedom of Information Act!

ALIEN COMMUNICATION

When I asked if we were still communicating with the visitors from the future, his answer was:

It has been attempted but communication is not of will.

Apparently, the aliens will only communicate on their terms. At Roswell, they must have communicated in order to regain some of their belongings. There are rumors that there have been other crashes of alien vehicles so I asked the question. Our guide replied:

Yes.

Were there other crashes at Corona?

There have been several.

Were the remains from the other crashes taken to Area 51? His answer was:

Yes.

No wonder they are keeping Area 51 such a secret! Next I said: So the government does not want us to know about the existence of extraterrestrials?

No, most will never know or believe.

I found that statement very disquieting. When I asked if the truth will ever come out, he replied:

Yes.

According to that answer, there is hope that the secrets of Roswell will become public knowledge.

DO YOU TRUST YOUR GOVERNMENT?

As we were finishing up our session, I considered what had happened to Secretary Forrestal when he wanted to bring out the truth about the aliens. I posed the question: "Is it safe for me to publicize the information that has been given during our sessions?" His answer did little to put my mind at ease. It was:

If you trust your government.

My answer to that question is obvious! I posed the question: Are you saying I should not publish this information? He replied:

Your choice.

I certainly wish he was a little more definitive. I attempted to push for an answer more to my liking. "I want the truth to come out. Will the heavenly spirits protect me?" I wasn't too happy with what he said next:

It goes deeper and it will not be without risk.

Great. I have enough trouble sleeping without dreaming about Men in Black. Next, I inquired if there would ever be a time when it would be safe. The master guide once again caught me off guard with his reply. It was:

It will alter the course of life.

I was having a hard time visualizing that my writing this book would be able to alter the course of life. His reply was:

No, what you will be opening up will.

I made a mental note to stay away from the 16th floor of hospitals or becoming part of another conspiracy theory.

REASON FOR SECRECY

A major outstanding question that remains to be answered for me is why the government went to such lengths to keep the existence of aliens from the public. When I asked the guide, he replied:

Mass hysteria.

One answer lies in how the public responded to a broadcast on the radio, years before the Roswell crash. On October 30, 1938, our government got a glimpse into how the American public would react to an alien attack. On this date, the Columbia Broadcasting System aired an adaptation of H. G. Wells novel *The War of the Worlds*, narrated by Orson Welles, over their radio network. The show was done in an unusual format for the times, the manner of a news broadcast. In spite of a disclaimer issued at the beginning of the show, many people panicked at the belief that we were being invaded by aliens from Mars. It was assumed by our government that release of information about a real alien encounter would create national panic. Hence one of the reasons for secrecy.

The advent of the Cold War brought another reason for secrecy. Russia's KGB infiltrated our population and government with spies. Even the CIA had been breached by the agents. Roswell provided a technology source that had the opportunity to sway the war in the favor of the Soviets if they gained access to the Roswell information. Our secret agencies would and did anything needed to preserve the technology for the United States. Why they still feel the need to maintain the secrecy of an event that happened over sixty years ago is a mystery to me.

THE IMPACT OF ROSWELL

In retrospect, the crash of the alien ship at Roswell may have been immensely important in the technological leaps that came after the incident. As stated by the guides, the information provided by the debris is still being studied today. Fiberoptic cables, so important to data transmission today, may have come from the strands of cable found in the debris. Laser technology was found in the small instruments on the alien craft. Unique and light-weight fabric materials were found in the wreckage. Little is known publicly from the autopsies, but it can be assumed that secret findings were used in research.

The heavenly guides' reservoir of knowledge is much greater than ours and, from my experience, the information is generally correct. Our guides gave us an incredible amount of information concerning the lengths our government has gone to in order to prevent the truth from being known about the existence of extraterrestrials and their interaction with our society.

The release of information in the form of literature written by participants in the event tend to prove the statement provided by the guides to be correct. For my part, if a man in a black suit knocks on my door, I am going to run out the back door as fast as possible. Unfortunately at my age, I can't move very fast.

CHAPTER 8

RENDLESHAM FOREST LIGHTS

L ocated in the county of Suffolk, near the town of Ipswich in Great Britain, the Rendlesham Forest lies between two Cold War secure NATO air bases that housed nuclear weapons. At the end of the chapter, I will tell the story of what really happened as told to us by our alien guide, Mou.

Two very detailed books have been written about the incident: *Left at East Gate* by Larry Warren and Peter Robbins and *Encounter in Rendlesham Forest* by Nick Pope. They give detailed information concerning the incident, as well as very detailed accounts of the events as stated by actual participants, and I rely heavily on these works for the accounts used in this chapter. I recommend these volumes for anyone interested in studying the event further. Not only do the authors describe the event, but they also describe the measures taken by the British and United States governments to keep the happening a secret.

What makes this event so interesting is that it was witnessed by both United States Air Force personnel and high-ranking British military officers. One of the most vociferous participants is the assistant base commander! The witnesses were emphatic in their testimony and gave written, sworn statements. The United States and British governments are just as emphatic in proving the events had no relationship to aliens. This is the stuff that makes for great alien conspiracy plots.

In late December 1980, things occurred over a three-day period that eventually caused the event to be referred to as Britain's Roswell. For those of you too young to remember the Cold War with the Soviet Union, let me start with a little historical background.

NUCLEAR-ARMED AND READY

At this point of the Cold War, the United States was renting the Woodbridge and Brentwaters air fields from Britain and using it as NATO facility for their aircraft. During this period, NATO considered the Soviet tank arsenal a great threat to roll across the plains of Europe, much like the Nazis had done a generation before. The bases held the A-10 close support aircraft that would be the first line of defense against a Soviet armored invasion.

Not only did the bases hold the close support aircraft, there were planes kept on the runway with fully armed nuclear weapons. In the event of a sneak attack, the planes could be in the air in minutes delivering a sudden nuclear strike. Needless to say, there was very strict security enforced on the bases. Any personnel protecting the bases underwent strict screening and had high-security clearances.

One of the individuals most outspoken about the events concerning the Rendlesham Forest incident was the assistant base commander, Colonel Charles Hart. A career officer, he served in Vietnam, Korea, and Japan before being assigned to Brentwaters RAF in 1980. He was promoted to base commander in 1984. He later served as director of the inspections directorate for the Department of Defense's inspector general before he retired in 1991. When you read his sworn affidavit and statements, you are reading information of personal experiences from one of the highest ranking members of the military to have ever gone public. By the end of the three-day occurrence in Rendlesham, many more highly qualified members of the armed forces were witnesses to the strange happenings. It took a monumental effort by the militaries of the United States and Great Britain to cover up the incident.

UNUSUAL EVENTS SEEN ON RADAR

Close radar surveillance was maintained around the bases during this period of the Cold War as Russian planes would test our defenses. Pilots were kept in the cockpit of fighters so they could be immediately dispatched. On an evening prior to the major UFO event, there had been strange sightings. Mal Scurrah was the radar operator on duty that evening and recorded the following statement about a strange vehicle that was recorded on the radar:

> We didn't have the faintest idea what it was. We checked through the air traffic agencies. There should have been nothing in that area at the time. The only thing we could do was send a jet aircraft in to find out what it was. They got to within about a quarter of a mile and the pilot suddenly started reporting that they could see a very bright light in the sky in front of them.
>
> It was stationary on the screen and then, in seconds, it moved off at a fantastic rate of speed. Within the space of five minutes, it was reaching 90,000 feet and higher and we lost it off the top end of the radar scope. There's nothing we have in this day that can perform those kind of maneuvers, the pilots wouldn't be able to take it.

The official statement is that there were no confirmed contacts on the radar during that time and all records have disappeared. The events taking place on that prior night were only just beginning.

LIGHTS IN THE FOREST

Around 3 a.m. on December 26, 1980, strange lights were reported descending into the forest near the East Gate of Woodbridge airfield by individuals guarding the base. A security patrol consisting of Staff Sargent Jim Penniston, Airman First Class John Burroughs, and Airman First Class Ed Cabansag was dispatched to investigate what they at first thought was a downed aircraft. They requested and were given permission to investigate the strange light.

As the team approached the light, they reported seeing a triangular-shaped craft, about the size of a tank, with small, large-headed beings. They were also aware of a variety of bright and colored lights. The security team observed the activity, and reported what they were observing over their walkie-talkies. As they were watching, the ship rose through the pines and took off.

When they returned to the post they filled out a log and were told to downplay the incident, especially not to use the term "UFO." These official logs are now missing. Shortly after the incident, participants were barred from discussing the facts and the event was designated "Top Secret." The witnesses' security clearances were upgraded to make the penalties for talking about the events much more serious.

According to those that have come forward, the men were debriefed and detained for several days. Some reported that the interrogators actually used drugs on the witnesses. Men in Black made it clear beyond any doubt that the events the men witnessed were not to become public knowledge. If the penalties were not considered stringent enough, one of the debriefers supposedly told the witnesses that "bullets are cheap."

As the years have passed and the participants are no longer members of the Armed Forces, they have come forward to tell their stories. The best way to describe the events are in the words of the participants. Sgt. Penniston describes the events that took place as follows:

THE STATEMENT OF STAFF SERGEANT JIM PENNISTON

As I mentioned before, Staff Sgt. Penniston was in charge of the three-man security team that was dispatched to initially investigate the mysterious lights in the forest. He tells the events of the first night as follows:

I received a call from the Control Centre to go on down to the East Gate and contact John Burroughs. And I asked them what was the nature of the problem down there and they said that they'd rather not tell me, they'd rather have me go down there and talk to the patrol man on the scene. The first thing that came to mind was an aircraft crash.

They notified me that they were tracking an unidentified bogey about 15 minutes ago and they confirmed it with contact with eastern radar and Heathrow in London and the approximate location was about 5 miles off base when they lost contact with it. It was Christmas time and there was no scheduled flying for that night. I got permission to proceed off base to investigate.

I started to see a defined shape and at that point I realized it wasn't an aircraft crash, a fire, or anything of that sort. The air was filled with electricity. You could feel it on your skin as we approached the object.

You felt like you were moving in slow motion, your hair on the back of your head was standing up, you felt like you had very little control over your body.

It was about the size of a tank, it was triangular in shape. Underneath the craft, was a high intensity white light emanating out of it and it was bordered by red and blue lighting, alternating.

On the upper left side of the craft, was an inscription. It measured six inches high, of symbols. They looked familiar, but I couldn't ascertain why.

It slowly started moving back, weaving in and around the trees... it raised up into the air and it shot off as fast as you could blink.[1] In 2014, Jim Penniston assisted in the publishing of *Encounters in Rendlesham Forest*. His statements can be reviewed in detail in that book.

Eyewitness Recalls Facts Under Hypnosis

As I mentioned before, Sergeant Penniston was in charge of the original security team. Troubled by the events, he attempted to refresh his recall of what actually took place. While undergoing regression hypnosis in 1994, Penniston subsequently claimed that the "craft" he encountered had come from our future, and was occupied by time travelers, not extraterrestrials. I covered the subject of aliens being time travelers from the future earlier in this book. According to our personal experiences with the spirit guides, much of what Sgt. Penniston disclosed under hypnosis appears to be accurate.

THE STATEMENT OF AIRMAN FIRST CLASS JOHN BURROUGHS

Airman First Class John Burroughs was also a member of the original security patrol. He recounts what happened when they approached the UFO either hovering or resting on three legs on the ground:

> The air was filled with electricity. You could feel it on your skin as we approached the object.
>
> On the upper left side of the craft, was an inscription. It measured six inches high, of symbols. They looked familiar, but I couldn't ascertain why.
>
> There were strange lights out in the forest. To me, it almost looked like Christmas lights at first, a Christmas display. At that point we looked at each other and we decided that we'd better go out and take a closer look 'cause we weren't sure what we were dealing with. What we were looking at wasn't real.

Burroughs also commented:

> You felt like you were moving in slow motion, your hair on the back of your head was standing up, you felt like you had very little control over your body.

As you can see from the statements of the participants, their bodies were affected by the presence of the alien ship. Both Penniston and Burroughs mention the fact that the air was filled with electricity and it was like they were moving in slow motion. Whatever abilities the aliens had, taking partial control of the airmen's bodies seemed to be part of it.

THE STATEMENT OF AIRMAN FIRST CLASS EDWARD CABANSAG

The third member of the original security team to investigate the site was Airman First Class Edward Cabansag. His version is quite interesting as his statements seem to be heavily influenced by his interrogations. His original report written on the morning of the incident has disappeared. The only copy of a statement under his name is on a blank sheet of paper that bears his signature but no date.

After the incident, he was interrogated and questioned at length about the events. He was given a retyped statement and was told to sign it without question and he would not have any future involvement with the case. The airman states that he signed the document that sanitized the incident and seemed to point to the fact that the lights were generated by a lighthouse several miles away and that it was signed under extreme duress. I have not printed that statement but it is available at www.therendleshamincident.com.

According to statement by Airman Cabansag's wife, he was threatened that bad things would happen if he made any statements about the incident. Apparently, he was interrogated for hours and intimidated into signing the statement. He has essentially remained out of the controversy. The Men in Black must have made quite an impression.

COLONEL HALT'S REPORT OF THE INCIDENT

The Deputy Base Commander at the Woodbridge Air Force Base, Lieutenant Colonel Charles Halt, responded to the reports and visited the location of the reported lights. On the first evening of the event, he did not see the lights, but inspected the landing area afterwards. Readings were taken with a Geiger counter of the depressions made by the UFO. The depressions showed a higher radioactivity than the surrounding area. The Colonel did oversee the reports written by the security team and suggested that they downplay the word UFO.

On the second night of the event, things would get up close and personal for Colonel Halt as he personally observed the alien ships and lights emitted from them. On the evening of December 27, he was attending a party on the base when one of the members of the security team entered the party and said, "They're back." Colonel Halt left the party and joined a security team to investigate what was happening. He carried a cassette tape recorder that was active during his investigation on that evening. The transcripts of his recorded conversations on that night are available with detail regarding what was being viewed by the investigating team at www.therendleshamforestincident.com/The_Full_Report.php.

As Halt attempted to investigate the happenings on the second evening, he involved other members of the military serving on the bases. Lights and generators were ordered to the area. Investigators used Geiger counters to check for radiation. By the end of the night, there were numerous witnesses to the strange happenings that had to be debriefed by the Ministry of Defense investigators.

In response to his personal experiences, on January 13, 1981, Col. Halt submitted a report to the British Ministry of Defense. It is now referred to in UFO conspiracy circles as the "Halt Memo." Here is the actual transcript of his memo. As you will see, it does not exactly reflect the statements made by the British government in later dispatches.

Colonel Charles Halt's report regarding the incident:

"Subject: Unexplained Lights
To: RAF/CC

Early in the morning of 27 Dec 80 (approximately 0300L), two USAF security police patrolmen saw unusual lights outside the back gate at RAF Woodbridge. Thinking an aircraft might have crashed or been forced down, they called for permission to go outside the gate to investigate. The on duty flight chief responded and allowed three patrolmen to proceed on foot. The individuals reported seeing a strange glowing object in the forest. The object was described as being metallic in appearance and triangular in shape, approximately two to three meters across the base and approximately two meters high. It illuminated the entire forest with a white light. The object itself had a pulsating red light on top and a bank(s) of blue lights underneath. The object was hovering or on three legs. As the patrolmen approached the object, it maneuvered through the trees and disappeared. At this time the animals on a nearby farm went into a frenzy. The object was briefly sighted approximately an hour later near the back gate."

[This was the part of the report that described what had been seen by the security team on the first evening. Halt's Report continued as he described the investigation of the landing site:]

2. "The next day, three depressions 1 1/2" deep and 7" in diameter were found where the object had been sighted on the ground. The following night the area was checked for radiation. Beta/Gamma readings of 0.1 milliroentgens were recorded with peak readings in the three depressions and near the center of the triangle formed by the depressions. A nearby tree had moderate (.05 – .07) readings on the side of the tree toward the depressions."

[Lt. Colonel Halt insisted that an appropriate entry be made in the security police log. But his report did not end there. The next night more activity occurred in Rendlesham Forest.]

3. "Later in the night a red sun-like light was seen through the trees. It moved about and pulsed. At one point it appeared to throw off glowing particles and then broke into five separate white objects and then disappeared. Immediately thereafter, three star-like objects were noticed in the sky, two objects to the north and one to the south, all of which were about 10° off the horizon. The objects moved rapidly in sharp angular movements and displayed red, green and blue lights. The objects to the north appeared to be elliptical through an 8–12 power lens. They then turned to full circles. The objects to the north remained in the sky for an hour or more. The object to the south was visible for two or three hours and beamed down a stream of light from time to time. Numerous individuals, including the undersigned [Halt himself], witnessed the activities in paragraphs 2 and 3."

[It is important to remember that this is not a statement by some man in the street. It was written and submitted by the deputy base commander. This was a man entrusted with nuclear weapons! Logically thinking, such a report could have endangered his military career. He had absolutely nothing to gain by telling the truth.]

Colonel Halt Notarizes His Conclusion in 2010

Colonel Halt retired from the Air Force in 1991. When his statement was released in 2001 under the Code of Practice for Access to Government Information (the forerunner of the Freedom of Information Act), needless to say he became quite famous in UFO circles. On June 17, 2010, he signed and notarized a statement in which he drew the following conclusion:

I believe the objects that I saw at close quarter were extraterrestrial in origin and that the security services of both the United States and the United Kingdom have attempted—both then and now—to subvert the significance of what occurred at Rendlesham Forest and RAF Brentwaters by the use of well-practiced methods of disinformation.

Not only is Colonel Halt stating that the occurrence he observed was alien in nature, but both the British and United States governments worked together to cover up the information! I know, it is very hard to believe that our government would knowingly mislead anyone.

BRITISH MEN IN BLACK

As the participants were to find out, the use of Men in Black is not only a United Stated phenomenon. The United States Department of Defense wanted no part of the controversy, even though the incident occurred in the vicinity of NATO bases controlled by US forces. Since the incident took place in the forest between the bases that was the property of Great Britain, the decision was made that it was a British problem. This decision did not prevent American radar records and documents from disappearing. As you will see, our government also assisted by purging personal records of our servicemen involved in the incident.

The accounts of the debriefing/interrogation/mind washing the men observing the events went through are quite troubling. Larry Warren tells of being drugged and brain washed for several days. He recounts being threatened to maintain his silence concerning the events. The story he tells reads like a bad spy novel.

At the prodding of his superiors he was given an honorable early discharge. He later attempted to reenlist only to find that his prior military records had essentially disappeared. He tried to access his records on multiple occasions only to find frustration. It was as if he had never served and there was certainly no way they were going to let him back in military service. Another witness to the event in the forest was so distraught that he subsequently allegedly committed suicide.

NEWSPAPERS GET THE STORY

On October 2, 1983, the proverbial cat got out of the bag. The bestselling Sunday newspaper in the United Kingdom, the *News of the World* printed a front page article stating that a UFO had landed, not crashed, in Suffolk.

Somehow the newspaper had gotten a copy of Colonel Halt's memo and decided to print the story for the world to see. Needless to say, the British Ministry of Defense was not overjoyed at the appearance of the newspaper article. On October 6, they released the following:

I can confirm that the Ministry of Defense did receive a report from base personnel of a UFO sighting near RAF Woodbridge on 27 December 1980. [This was the report published by the *News of the World* on Oct. 2 1983.] The report was dealt with in accordance with normal procedures, i.e., it was passed to staff concerned with air defense matters who examine such reports to satisfy themselves that there are no defense implications. In this instance the Ministry of Defense was satisfied that there was nothing of defense interest in the alleged sightings. There was no question of any contact with "alien beings."

The *News of the World* newspaper proclaims a UFO landed in England. Public Domain.

Notice that they did not say there wasn't any incident, only that there were no defense implications. I guess having a UFO fly over a nuclear arsenal unimpeded did not have defense implications! The British government has remained steadfast in denying the events that took place on that cold night in 1980. Ufologists have been just as determined in their attempts to prove that a true alien occurrence took place.

WHAT REALLY HAPPENED

The documentation concerning the Rendlesham incident is unique in its detail. With all the books that have been written and certified statements, it is difficult to see how the government could be advertising such a different explanation of what took place. We used our gift of spirit communication to sort out what really took place. During a session in September 2014, we asked questions about the incident while channeling on Skype with our associates K and Doc in Salt Lake City. Mou and his friends were very anxious to discuss what really happened.

I started off by asking the most obvious question: Did aliens land in Rendlesham Forest in 1980. He replied:

Yes.

Thank goodness for that answer; I could have wasted an awful lot of work and research had his answer been different. Next I inquired if more than one UFO was involved in the incident and he answered:

4

At this point of the interview, the information was pretty much in line with the written statements. There were a lot of guesses why the ship chose that particular spot to land. When I asked, the answer was a lot simpler than I expected.

A breakdown of one ship.

The witnesses did say it looked like the aliens were working on the vehicle. I reworded the question and asked the purpose of the alien mission.

To fix a disabled ship.

The books laid out a theory that they were observing the NATO bases because of the nuclear weapons that were stored there. When I asked if the weapons had anything to do with the appearance of the aliens, the answer was:

Nope. One ship lost power. We sent our mechanics in with parts. The other two ships were making a cover for the tow ships. When it was fixed, we all got out of there.

I guess when you are an extraterrestrial, you can't just call AAA when your vehicle breaks down. The whole event at Rendlesham Forest simply was caused by one of the UFOs suffering a mechanical breakdown! I was amazed at how similar their problems are to our own. The reports of the observers stated that there was a beam of light that covered the area. When I asked if the beam of light was some type of weapon, Mou answered:

> *No. It was an energy booster from the*
> *mothership. A jump of sorts.*

That was an answer I was not expecting! My follow up statement was: Are you saying the damaged ship needed a jump start from the mother ship? His answer was:

> *Right.*

Where we use jumper cables, they use beams of light! So much for all the complicated theories of what was taking place during the event, they were just trying to repair their small space ship. The reports also described a pulsating light that broke into five smaller lights. When I asked what that was all about, there was also a simple answer.

> *A flare we have.*

Since we were on the subject of their vehicles, I though a couple of questions concerning details of their flying machines would be in order. Next, I inquired as to how many aliens were in the mothership.

> *The mothership holds around 200.*
> *Each small ship holds from 4 to 9.*

What is the minimum it takes to fly the small ships?

> *4. A pilot, sub-pilot, navigator, and engineer.*

I commented that it sounds a lot like one of our flight crews.

> *Except for the engineer. The engineer*
> *plays with our motors more.*

Larry Warren, in his book, makes some pretty wild claims surrounding the incident, one of which he talks about viewing an underground area under the

NATO base where he observed aliens and humans working together. When I asked the guide if such an area really existed, his answer was:

Yes, still does.

The books about the incident tell stories of Men in Black telling the participants such things (as mentioned earlier) like "bullets are cheap" and witnesses committing suicide. I asked if agents killed anyone to keep them quiet about the incident. His answer did not do a lot to quiet my nerves.

Ha, ha, ha, ha.

I was beginning to think that aliens have a very perverse sense of humor. I pressed the question and asked what he thought was so funny.

It was against your agreements.
Have other ways they were told to use.

Our visitors from outer space seem to have a higher regard for incarnate life than our own institutions. In 1987, the area of the incident was hit by a gigantic storm that destroyed much of the trees that showed the evidence that something out of the ordinary had taken place. The storm was so non-typical of the area that conspiracy theorists suggested man-made manipulation of the weather to destroy evidence. When I posed the possibility of human interference Mou replied:

Not natural.

My follow up inquired if the storm was man made. Once again the answer was not what I expected.

No, us made.

I knew from other sessions that our government could manipulate the weather, but was not aware extraterrestrials could do the same. Their abilities seem to be almost unlimited.

When you compare the written statements of the participants in the event, there is a marked similarity between their words and the facts given us by Mou. In the case of the Rendlesham Forest Lights, the printed truth was out there, it just took the words of a friendly alien to prove it.

A DISTINCT SIMILARITY

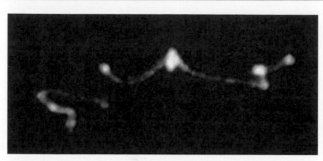

A photograph of the lights at Rendlesham Forest. Public Domain.

While taking the photography for my first book, I recorded many images that could not be identified. While doing the research for this chapter, I came across the picture image shown on the left that is said to be taken during the Rendlesham Forest event. It is a bit grainy but you can get the general idea of the appearance of the lights.

In my chapter on personal encounters I included several pictures of lights taken over the Gettysburg Battlefield in Pennsylvania. When I found the above picture on the Internet under Rendlesham Forest pictures, I thought the image looked remarkably familiar. On the night, in 2010, when I took these pictures I actually shot eight frames that showed the mysterious lights in the sky. The pictures were taken at twilight and my shutter speed was 1/60 of a second so whatever it was, the light was traveling at a high rate of speed. In the photo on the next page, you can see the close-up images. As you can see, there is a marked similarity in my personal pictures and the one attributed to the Rendlesham Forest event.

The Rendlesham Forest Lights certainly appear to be one of the best documented alien events that has been brought to public attention. It would be interesting to see some of the actual photographs that were taken at the time of the incident, but they are either hidden or destroyed.

The more I researched this event the more I realized the extent of the hiding of the facts by our governments. I asked Mou, in the opinion of the aliens, what event represented the greatest cover up of any of the major alien occurrence that had taken place. He answered:

The one in England. They had to really spin the story. They were caught by surprise.

Our alien friends consider the Rendlesham Forest Lights incident the most important cover up of all the events that have taken place. As more and more individuals come forward to corroborate the published events, maybe the light

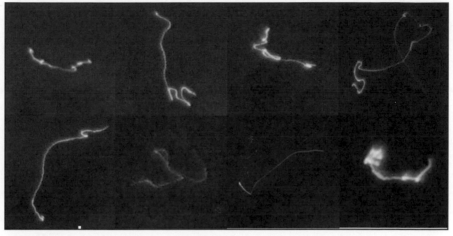

Eight photographs of the same type of lights seen at Rendlesham Forest, taken in Gettysburg, Pennsylvania. Courtesy author.

of truth will shine on the governments of the United States and Great Britain and they will actually release the true documents and facts of the event. From all the statements given to us by the guides, my guess is the odds of us finding the truth is about the same as the odds of hell freezing over.

CHAPTER 9

OPERATION HIGH JUMP

The more I read about this next event that took place in 1947, the more I realized that it deserved to be a chapter of its own. It is an occurrence that involves a United States military task force, the rumor of alien combat, a Nazi secret base in Antarctica, and a cover up of the facts by our government. In addition to all that, there is also the possibility of the assassination of high officials to keep the events from the public. Operation High Jump, led by the famous Admiral Byrd, certainly has all the components of a great alien conspiracy.

AN AMERICAN HERO

Admiral Richard E. Byrd was a true American hero. He led expeditions to the North and South Poles and was a pioneer in early American aviation. In 1926, during a fifteen-hour flight, he was the first to fly over the North Pole. For this feat, he was awarded the United States Medal of Honor. (Keep in mind this was before the days of pressurized cabins.) By 1929, he obtained the rank of rear admiral and held this rank throughout World War II. His familiarity with the continent of Antarctica was probably the reason he was selected to lead Operation High Jump.

When I asked our alien guide, Mou, if Admiral Byrd came into contact with aliens during Operation High Jump, he replied:

Yes.

The next question got to the heart of the matter. Did our task force in Operation High Jump get into a fight with aliens?

Yes, a misunderstanding. It ended friendly.

That answer certainly aroused my curiosity. There are rumors that there was armed confrontation between the task force and the aliens. When I asked if any aliens were killed during the misunderstanding the answer was:

No.

When I asked if any of the American task force were killed, he gave a different answer.

By miscommunication, yes.

In all my research, this is the first time I actually heard evidence of aliens and American forces in armed combat. Needless to say, I had a lot more questions for my alien friend. With you knowing in advance that our task force came into contact with aliens, let me give a little historical background so you can better understand the events. I know that I'd never heard of Operation High Jump before conducting the research for this book. My guess is you will find this chain of events very intriguing.

SOME HISTORY

ALIENS CRASH IN BAVARIA

In 1938, an incident took place that was to have a large influence on the Nazi research into extraterrestrial technology. There is a rumor that a UFO crashed in

Bavaria in which members of the alien crew survived. While there is no conclusive, published evidence, it is believed that the engine of the crashed vehicle was pretty much intact and provided the basis for the Germans to attempt to build a saucer-shaped vehicle from reverse engineering the wreckage. I asked Mou if a UFO actually did crash in Bavaria in 1938. His reply was short and verified the rumors.

Yes.

My next question was if any of the alien crew members survived the crash.

2.

We have been told that there are many different types of aliens, so I inquired what nature of extraterrestrials were involved in the accident.

They were shape shifters.

The Nazis got lucky on that incident. Shape shifters look like humans and would be very easy to conceal from the public. If they had been from Mou's planet, they would have been working with blue-skinned individuals standing over nine feet that would probably stand out in a crowd. I knew from previous sessions that aliens had assisted the Nazi war effort in the beginning, so I inquired if this crash was the foundation for the initial cooperation of aliens. He replied in the affirmative.

Yes.

The German scientists were trying to perfect a flying saucer, so I asked if this crash provided the initial scientific knowledge for this effort. He answered:

Started to.

I had seen pictures on the Internet of flying saucers with the Nazi insignia on them. My next inquiry focused on if they really were trying to make a flying saucer.

They were trying this on their own after seeing ours.

I asked what happened to the shape shifters that were working with the Germans; he stated:

They were rescued before it was working.

A BAD DECISION

When Hitler took control of the German government in 1933, many of the Jewish scientists who would prove so critical to our nuclear program fled Europe. As the war progressed, many of the remaining scientists were conscripted into the Nazi army to replace the depleted manpower. In spite of all these problems, it is believed that Germany was actually the first to explode a type of nuclear weapon on March 4, 1945. This success points to some kind of outside help with nuclear technology. With their advanced technology, it was rumored that they must have had the assistance of extraterrestrial mentors. When I posed the question to Mou, he replied:

This is why you hired the Nazi scientists. They were instructed by us.

I was having a bit of trouble believing that the aliens chose to help Nazi Germany to obtain a weapon of mass destruction. I tried to clarify the question by asking specifically if they helped the German scientists to make an atomic bomb. He answered truthfully:

Yes, our big mistake.

Next, I inquired if there was a Nazi base in Antarctica and he also said:

Yes.

If the Germans went to all the effort of creating a base in the harshest environment on Earth, it is a safe bet that whatever they were doing, they wanted to keep it a secret. When I asked the purpose of the base the answer was:

Atom splitting.

Rumors abound about the nuclear program of the German war machine. I had heard about their experiments with heavy water, but never realized just how close they were to exploding a bomb. I asked Mou if the Nazis ever exploded a nuclear weapon.

Yes. Three tests. The first was no good. The other two were good. They had plans to put them on war heads but had to figure out how to make it light and less bulky. The USA instead of worrying about size, built planes around the bomb.

The idea that Hitler's Germany actually conducted successful tests of an atom bomb is quite frightening. I guess this is a case where size really did matter. If President Truman suspected there was a possibility that surviving Nazis in Antarctica were working on nuclear weapons, you can understand why such a massive task force would be sent to investigate.

NAZIS IN ANTARCTICA

Adding to the intrigue, there was a rumor that a large flotilla of German submarines and many high-ranking scientists were missing. It was said that as many as ten submarines had left Germany packed with the personal belongings of these high-ranking Nazis. Three of the subs were traced to Argentina, a country friendly to the Germans, but the rest were out there *somewhere*. It is a good guess that Operation High Jump was ready to deal with more than penguins. When I asked if there was a Nazi sub base in Antarctica I was told the following.

They had one there but we stopped it. It interfered with us. This is where things began to go bad between their government and us.

What happened after things started to go bad between the Nazi and aliens?

After the treaty, we destroyed the base.

I asked if we had made a treaty with the aliens during World War II.

Yes, treaty. We would not interfere on either side. Hitler had help. Backed off after hearing what he said.

Alien assistance is probably the reason for some of the early success of the Third Reich.

INVASION OF ANTARCTICA

Upon the destruction of the German war machine in Europe, the attention of the Allies was directed toward the Soviet Union as Stalin continued to gain control of Europe. In spite of their aggression, in 1946–1947, the United States created a task force with the official name "The United States Navy Antarctic Developments Program" under the command of retired Admiral Richard E. Byrd Jr. to be dispatched to Antarctica. This was no small operation; it consisted of thirteen ships, 4,700 men, and multiple aircraft.

The flagship for the operation was the USS *Mount Olympus*, a floating command post with combat information spaces—a ship designed for a landing force commander during a large amphibious landing operation: an aircraft carrier, the USS *Philippine*, thirteen Navy support ships, six flying boats, six helicopters, along with two seaplane tenders, and fifteen other aircraft. It definitely seems like a lot of equipment to do a little exploring. The primary mission was officially said to establish a research base that would be named Little America. In retrospect, it does seem a bit strange our government would dedicate such resources to Antarctic research, especially with the rise of Communist Russia.

We had been told that the Admiral had a misunderstanding with the aliens. When I asked Mou to clarify what he meant, this was his statement.

I guess he thought someone beat him there. We showed him he was the first human but not the first. We were first.

I thought I would clarify the statement about the Admiral being afraid someone beat him. When I asked him to clarify what he meant he went into detail.

His ego was very out of control. He was going to neutralize anyone who got ahead of him. When he saw beings ahead of him, he concluded he was not the first. He was in fear of not being the best explorer in history. So he fired on the aliens. The aliens shot them with a stun force until they could understand the situation.

I could see why it was probably not a good idea to fire first at aliens. The admiral was lucky they only u ed a stun force.

A SECRET DIARY

Conspiracy theorists believe that a secret diary, supposedly written in 1947 by Admiral Bryd, told of a secret meeting between aliens and the admiral in an underground city. According to the diary, on February 19, 1947, he was making an exploratory flight when his airplane was taken over by a strange force. They were taken to a odd underground city, known as the Inner World of the Earth, where a civilization far more advanced than humans thrived. Their leader warned that humans had reached the point of no return and the dangers of nuclear weapons would destroy the earth if left unchecked. He stated that the recent war with the use of nuclear weapons on Japan was only a prelude of things to come. Byrd was told to return to the surface and carry this message to his leaders.

By March 11, he was back at the Pentagon where he apparently relayed his message and it was passed on to the president. As a result, he was interviewed by Top Security Forces and a medical team and placed under national security provisions, where he was ordered to remain silent in regard to all that he had learned on behalf of humanity. As he grew older, he found it more difficult to keep the secrets as indicated by a final entry in his diary on December 24, 1956.

Admiral Byrd died on March 11, 1957, supposedly in his sleep from a heart attack. Conspiracy theorists believe that he was killed to keep that information from becoming public. When I asked Mou if there was really a city under the Earth he replied:

> *This is where they took him to heal and talk.*
> *The group was cold, hungry, and sleep deprived.*
> *They stayed there about a week.*

So most of what he wrote in his secret diary is true?

> *Most, yes. There is some he wrote while*
> *being sleep deprived but most is fact.*

According to both Admiral Byrd and Mou there is a city under the earth that is still occupied by very advanced aliens. All the hollow Earth enthusiasts must be quite happy to hear that.

DEAD MEN TELL NO TALES

During the time of the Roswell incident and Operation High Jump, James Forrestal was the Secretary of the Navy. If you remember, I pointed out that he committed "suicide" while trying to hang himself out a 16th floor window of Bethesda Naval Hospital. I asked Mou if Secretary Forrestal was murdered and his answer was:

> *Yes, we did not know.*

There is also a mystery surrounding the death of Admiral Byrd. It seems that having knowledge of extraterrestrials can be injurious to your health. During one of our sessions with the alien spirit I inquired if Admiral Byrd was killed to keep him from disclosing information about extraterrestrials. His reply was:

Yes.

STILL OPERATING IN ANTARCTICA

It seems as though the continent of Antarctica is a very popular location for the construction of bases, by both humans and aliens. When I inquired if aliens still operate a base there the answer was:

Yes.

When I asked if the base was just used by aliens, he replied:

No, it is shared. Another will be made.

Not only is there a current facility being used by aliens and humans, there is another one in the works.

In 1979, there is evidence that a nuclear test was set off on the continent of Antarctica. At that time, we had a satellite specifically designed to check for violations of the existing nuclear test-ban treaty. Apparently, a nuclear blast gives off a distinctive double flash of light—a rapid flash on detonation followed by a longer flash. On September 22 of that year, our satellite recorded such a double flash over the southern continent. Our government has discredited the reports, blaming it on bad readings from an aging satellite.

NUCLEAR TESTS IN ANTARCTICA

In one of our earlier sessions, Mou had stated that there were nuclear tests conducted over Antarctica. When I asked him who set off the blasts, he answered:

Russia. Gray collaboration. They were studying above ground blasts and the ability to harm the force to neutralize a bigger blast. The thinking was above ground blast will take the force out of a ground blast by robbing the needed reactions out of the air. To have a correct blast the chemicals in the air must have its components to work to optimum so if you pre blast the nitrogen, next blasts will be duds. Small damage, less fall out. The first blast if small will be less damage and it saves infrastructure and people.

I guess I should have asked him why the Grays were working with Russia, but I could not get over his knowledge about nuclear fusion. It was like I was talking to a nuclear scientist.

The implications of Operation High Jump are quite extensive. It ranged from actual military interaction with aliens to Admiral Byrd being personally introduced to a hidden city under the surface of the Earth. Our government once again seems to have exerted extreme measures to keep the information from the public. It seems as though many humans and aliens have a voracious appetite for the southern exposure of the Antarctic climate and activities there will probably end no time soon.

CHAPTER 10

CONVERSATIONS WITH AN ALIEN SPIRIT

Hopefully by this point of the book, you will have come to the same conclusion that I have: namely that aliens really do exist. If you are still having a problem with that concept, you are really going to have a problem with this chapter. Yes folks, this chapter is based entirely on direct communication with the spirit of an alien! I would also like to warn you that he gave us information that many people might not be willing to accept or even be willing to hear. In the previous chapters, I used quotes from my alien spirit friend to answer many instances of alien activity. This chapter is entirely devoted to conversations with Mou. All I am doing is passing on what we are being told. You have to decide for yourself if you believe it or not.

During the summer of 2014, we were channeling in Salt Lake and I asked the guides questions about what would be taking place in the future. At the time, their answer did not seem to make a lot of sense. It was:

We cannot wait for your more.
We are sure you will love as much.

In retrospect, I think they were talking about being able to communicate with an actual alien spirit. They were correct. I love what is taking place and what we are learning as much as what has taken place in the past.

If you have read my previous book, I discuss the idea that many of the events in your life are preordained. As I was to find out, the idea of writing a book about aliens was probably planted in my mind by the spirit guides. Actually it was probably planted in my mind by an alien guide. In my first contact with Mou, he said:

I want to write two more.

Somehow I think I am very involved with that statement. Who knew that aliens could be authors with a little human assistance? I know I am repeating myself, but I have to mention that I have the video and audio proof on file to prove that what you are about to read really happened. The words of Mou are taken directly, word for word, from the audio portion of the recordings.

ALIENS HAVE SOULS, TOO

Prior to this time, it never really occurred to me that an alien would have a soul, similar to those of human beings. The thought of our heaven being occupied by creatures from another planet may seem a bit strange. However, another way of looking at our world would be that an alien might think it a bit strange that their heaven is occupied by the souls of humans. This whole concept was introduced to us during a channeling session in Salt Lake City with our clairvoyant friends, K and Doc. I had commented to the guide that there was a lot I did not understand about aliens and said that I could not write about something I did not understand. He replied:

No one does. So we are going to teach you. They are like worm holes. They have entrances in different places and you can travel thru them. We are going to dictate most of it or we should say a new teacher. Yes. His name is Mou.

I thought that was a really strange name for a guide, but have learned from experience that we are being led down a learning path. Strange name or not, I was quite anxious to meet him. When I asked how soon I could meet him the answer was:

Get through with these projects.

At the time of the session, I was considering combining this alien book with another one about historical conspiracies that is about half finished. When I asked the guide if I should keep this book separate, he ducked the question, but said something that really caught my attention.

Mou is good at that subject; he is one.

My ears definitely perked up at that answer. Not sure that I had heard the guide correctly, I followed up by asking if my new guide was going to be an alien. The answer was short and to the point.

Yes.

The fact that we were going to have an alien for a spirit guide was pretty far out there, even for me. I replied, "I would love to meet him." His answer indicated that guides have a pretty good sense of humor. It was:

He is dead. Ha, Ha, Ha. Mou will need to learn
this [the channeling board]. He will begin to talk with
you. Most UFOs are from different dimensions.

The thought of being introduced to an actual alien, even though it would be a spirit, was a bit overwhelming. I asked if Mou would appear to both Connie and me.

Yes. No abductions.

I must admit that put my mind at ease. At least I would not be seeing a UFO from the inside! As you will see in the chapter on personal encounters, he actually did appear to me and confirmed his appearance in a later session.

MEETING MOU

The next week, Connie and I had to return from the Salt Lake area to our business in Pennsylvania, leaving a 2,000-mile distance between us and K and Doc. At the last session we held in Salt Lake City before heading back east, the guides suggested we use Skype to communicate and channel. Knowing a good idea when I hear one, we decided to attempt long-distance channeling and set up the necessary connection. By the end of September 2014, we were ready to talk to the guides using video communication and the Internet. Needless to say, I was quite anxious to try to reach Mou. When we began the session, I asked if our new alien guide was present. He was not only present, he was more than ready to communicate.

OK. I am here because you called me.
When you write, about an hour before you need to call me.
This way I can get into your eyes and see what you write. If I
do not like what you say or the way you say it, I can give you a
sign, like an itchy nose or blurry eyes. I am certain we
will be as one. I wish to write two more.

Apparently, we were going to become really good friends! I hadn't, however, realized he was going to censor my writing. It is times like this that I wonder just how much control we really have over our lives. No doubt I was going to find out. As the session progressed, I thought I would ask him some personal questions.

The idea to write a book on aliens seemed very foreign to the path our previous channeling sessions had been taking. I asked Mou if he had planted the idea to write this book in my head.

No, but I jumped on the idea when asked by your guide.

Notice he did not say my guide didn't plant the idea. Since that first long-distance Skype session, whenever I am transcribing the session notes and working on the chapters in the book, I have the feeling that I am getting some help. The next time we channeled, I asked him if he was helping me work on the notes and write. His answer really caught me off guard:

And enjoying your mind too. I was.

We almost lost Connie when she copied the "enjoying your mind" part. After being together for over fifty years, there are many time she finds it inconceivable that anyone could enjoy my mind. I think I can also include my daughters on that list.

Deciding that maybe it would be better to change the subject, I asked him if there were currently many different types of aliens here on earth. His reply confirmed my suspicions.

Oh, many. Yes.

I followed up by asking if they were from many different planets. He responded:

Yes, I have friends from 12 other planets.

He must be a very friendly spirit to have so many extraterrestrial friends on the other side and from such scattered locations.

A LONG WAY FROM HOME

Not only do aliens exist, they seem to be quite plentiful and from all over the galaxy. After a lead in like that, I had to ask what planet he came from. Once again, his answer far exceeded expectations.

Out on the farthest arm of the Milky Way, on the tip there is a planet the size of your Jupiter. It has 8 moons and twin suns. We breathe a nitrogen rich gas. We are tall and thin. We live mostly subsurface but our food grows on land. Water is not like yours. It is most of all below. Every morning it rains.

I thought he was going to be from our Solar System, but the farthest arm of the Milky Way is one hell of a commute in rush hour. A lot of other questions came to mind, like: What kind of a sunset do you have when there are two suns or how many phases of the moon are there when there are eight moons? But they would have to wait for another day.

YOU ARE GOING TO MEET A TALL BLUE STRANGER

If you watch the alien programs on television, you get the idea that our guests from other planets are gray in color and have very large eyes. I asked our new acquaintance from outer space what he looked like when he had a body.

Tall, thin with large eyes and a bluish skin. Small ears and small nose, big mouth. Hands have four fingers and a thumb like yours. And our feet are the same. Our feet are hands. You cannot tell sexes by looking. On our planet we walk or ride energy streams. To fly almost all crafts look alike. It is because it is the most effective method. I do not reinvent the world.

I doubt even the most imaginative reader could have anticipated that answer. If his feet are hands, it would seem that he has four hands, two of which are feet, or vice versa. It certainly does not meet the well-publicized profile of aliens with which we are familiar. He said he was tall, so I thought I would find out just how tall my new friend was in life.

In your measurements just over 9 feet tall.

He would definitely stand out in a crowd. I asked him how long aliens lived. I found his answer a little depressing.

Each being has its own genetic clock.
Yours is really short. One of the shortest.

I guess when God was determining how long humans would live, he decided to keep it short, so we could only screw up so much in a lifetime. With everything that is happening, I can't say that I blame him. Being curious as to how long my new friend actually had an incarnate life, I asked for more details.

We live your time about 1,000 years.
We are not adults until we are 300.

The vision of potty training for 100 years entered my mind, but I made the decision to keep my mouth shut. Next I inquired when he passed in our time.

1987.

He had mentioned that the average lifespan on his planet was about 1,000 years, so I inquired how old he was when he passed.

In your time I was 942. My planet 159. Our rotation around
two suns is much longer. We have twin stars as our suns.

I felt sorry that he passed at such a young age. It is hard to imagine a lifespan ten times longer than our own.

ALL ABOUT ROBBE

He had already described his home planet, so I asked if it had a name.

We call it Robbe.

He has also said that the water on his planet was different than ours.

$H3O$. Heavier. Does not freeze in low temps.
It has to drop pretty cold to freeze.

I guess that answers the question if they have snow on Robbe. If it doesn't freeze, there cannot be snow as we know it. I thought I would make one last personal inquiry, so I asked him how many wives he had.

3, ha ha ha. On my planet males are born less often.
About 1 to 5. This way less food and things are used.

I could not help wondering what it was like to live for 1,000 years being outnumbered by women five to one. My next question was if there were any aliens that looked like humans.

There are two that shape change. They can
morph to look like you. All others need to hide.

I guess I have to stop kidding my granddaughters about how ridiculous the television concept of shape shifters are. The idea that the aliens occupy the same Heaven as humans seemed a little odd. I thought I would verify it by asking whether or not, when aliens die, they really do go to the same areas of heaven as humans.

It depends. Yes. If we are from the Milky Way, we have the
same God and thus we go to the same Heaven. If we are from a
different God we go to that Heaven. Heavens are just for the
living. Once we progress out of Heaven, we can go anywhere.

I had never heard before that different galaxies had different Gods and each God was responsible for his own Heaven. That thought is going to take a little while to sink in. On a related subject, I asked Mou if aliens reincarnate the same as humans.

Just like you. Yes.

The circle of life is indeed universal. I know from our other experiences that the soul makes its own decision when it wants to reincarnate and return for another life path. I asked if an alien soul also makes its own decision to return.

Just like you, but other Gods have other rules
so if you are from other Gods, you do it that God's way.
Generally speaking, we all are doing the same growing.
Some live 1,000 years so reincarnation is slower because only
so many souls can live at a time. There must be a certain
energy away from God at a time.

It was starting to look like the life and soul experiences of aliens were very much like those of humans. It takes multiple lifetimes to gain soul experience. I guess to the extraterrestrials, we are the aliens. The concept of God is intergalactic.

AN ORDERLY GALAXY

Getting back to the fact that Mou had friends from twelve planets, I was curious why they would want to come to our little planet. When asked the purpose of their visits to Earth, his reply was:

Observing, friends, we all have our motives.
About half interact. Two are watching only.

With all these visitors to earth, I figured there must be some type of order out there. His next answer addressed that subject.

All have to go thru the inter-planet committee to visit. We are
not free to interfere. Advanced places are governed by a
committee. We have to get ok to play on the planets with life.

Notice that he said advanced places are governed by a committee. That certainly excludes earth. I was starting to get the impression that in the well-organized galaxy, earthlings were not too highly regarded. He had just said that advanced places were governed by a committee. His statement implied an efficiency and coordination of governmental procedures unknown on our planet. It crossed my mind that we would be defenseless from an advanced civilization that wished us harm.

In our movies, aliens are always fighting with someone. When I asked if extraterrestrials ever fight each other, Mou said:

> *We did at one time. This is why the committee was formed.*
> *Now there is not much disagreement.*

Can you imagine a community so large that has little disagreement? No wonder aliens want to come here to observe humans. I asked if there were any unfriendly aliens.

> *Yes, we keep them away. They cannot gain permission to visit.*

You can assume from that statement that there are no aliens here on Earth that we have to fear.

GALACTIC LAW AND ORDER OR ELSE

It was more and more apparent that the advanced alien cultures were regarding earthlings as youngsters that had to be protected from intergalactic bullies. The governing committee must have some powerful influence to enforce their will among the varied galactic cultures.

I inquired what happens if anyone went against the orders of the governing committee. He answered:

> *They are punished by sanctions and expelled*
> *until they pay back the committee with gifts for all the planets.*
> *A costly mistake. Yours is not the only planet we have*
> *restrictions on. There are thousands.*

The idea that a committee billions of miles away from Earth would know if one of their visitors violated the rules is a concept that should be learned by our police departments. I asked Mou how the committee knew if someone broke the rules.

We have devices like cameras they must carry
at all times. So an alarm goes off if someone breaks a
rule. If you choose to visit a planet you agree to follow
protocol. This device monitors your feelings.

It sounds like the governing body of the galaxies is quite serious about protecting our young life forms here on Earth. I guess if they let anything happen to us, they wouldn't have anywhere to go on vacation. The Committee sounds like an intergalactic United Nations, but in this case they really accomplish something.

PROTECTING HUMANS

I tried to advance the conversation by asking if the visitors from outer space attempted to affect our historical outcomes.

Mostly we just watch, but sometimes our hearts
take over. Mostly small things, but sometimes big things.
If we intervene too much, we lose our visit.

I asked for an example where the aliens intervened to protect our planet. His answer was:

When harm is at hand like the missile thing on Cuba.

For those of you who are too young to remember, in 1962, at the height of the Cold War, Russian leader Nikita Khrushchev attempted to arm Communist-controlled Cuba with nuclear weapons. President Jack Kennedy ordered a naval blockade to stop the ships carrying the missiles and that the facilities in Cuba be dismantled. In essence, negotiations led to the Soviet Union backing down and removing the weapons. This was probably the closest our nation ever came to nuclear war. I asked what the aliens did to help resolve the matter.

We warned Russia to back off or we will make you.

I could only guess what the term "make you" meant. The more we communicated, the more I realized just how much influence aliens have had over our safety and development.

It was beginning to sound like it was standing room only for the extraterrestrials observing the human species on our planet. I asked him if, when he was in body form, he'd ever visited Earth.

Twice.

At least he was speaking from personal experience. I asked what the purpose for his visits was.

Pick up a stranded team and one to take needed supplies. One took about a month and one I stayed for about 10 years.

It appears that our planet did not impress Mou enough that he decided to take up residence on Earth.

VIOLENCE AND WARS ON EARTH

I thought I would ask what the aliens thought about our violence and wars.

You are a young people and you have much to settle and learn. As young planets go, you are rather peaceful. Other planets are more hostile, but some are peaceful.

If Earth is rather peaceful, I can't imagine what the other planets are like! I went on to inquire if humans are considered a lower form of life by our intergalactic visitors.

No, just young.

That was a bit of a relief. At least they didn't look down on us as lower life forms, just as adults would regard the acts of young children. Judging from what is going on in our current world, I find it unimaginable that cultures can get along. Not much doubt that humans have a lot of growing up to do.

A VERY RAPID TRANSIT SYSTEM

I was having a very hard time figuring out how they could travel from the far reaches of the Milky Way in such short periods of time. The only method of travel I had ever heard of (on television) was by using a worm hole—whatever that was. I asked Mou if aliens used worm holes.

> *This is the best way but not the only way. My favorite way is like an energy to ride. It gets me places faster.*

I'd never heard of riding an energy. When we asked about it, his answer opened the way to a lot more questions.

> *It is faster than light. It is time reversing. You will have to talk to someone smarter than me to explain the math. Your energy to return and go happens all over the space continuum. They are a vortex. Each only come close to where you want to go. And you jump in and out of them where you want to go. Where worm holes are right where you are going to return and to search closely. Worm holes can collapse on you cutting off your gate. Vortexes are more stable and if one ends you just wait to jump another.*

That certainly covered a lot of information, none of which I really understood! He had talked about worm holes a lot, so I thought I would ask just what a worm hole really was.

> *OK. The space that looks empty to you is really filled with a fluid-like substance, yet solid, and the nature that rules it makes things in it. It is like a tunnel and you can get in one of these things and time speeds up. You can move faster than light, because time rules speed so there are no limits. Since there is no time you do not age and you go from one place to the next with ease. But they can collapse on you.*

And I thought I was mixed up before I asked the question. I have a lot more questions about this subject but they will have to wait. We asked him how long it takes to get from his planet on the far arm of the Milky Way to earth.

> *About ten hours if all is perfect. Remember once you hit more than light speed, time reverses.*

My guess is the hard part is hitting light speed. It never occurred to me that time reversed when you exceed the speed of light. Actually, I never thought it would be possible to exceed the speed of light. These guys can cross the entire galaxy in the same time it takes us to drive from central Pennsylvania to Chicago!

WHO'S YOUR GRANDDADDY?

I read somewhere that Albert Einstein had commented that time would reverse when you exceeded the speed of light. As if he was reading my mind, which he usually does, he made another comment:

> *Albert Einstein was a high bred. Grandfather*
> *on mom's side was a star man.*

That statement was really a low blow for the human race. We can't even take credit for one of our most brilliant scientists. One of his grandfathers was an alien! I guess that takes off a lot pressure over asking if aliens and humans ever have sex. When Mou said there were extraterrestrials that could morph to look like humans, he really wasn't kidding. My next question inquired if his grandmother knew she married a star man.

> *Yes, but no one else.*

I have no idea how you keep something like that a secret. I was intrigued by how a star man could marry a human and no one would notice. Next, I inquired what a star man was. I think he kind of ducked the question.

> *Individual closer to you on the same arm.*

He was referring to an arm of the Milky Way. Not able to let the subject drop, I asked if a star man assumed the form of a human.

> *His planet looked like yours. It is like two*
> *animals breeding. Like a tiger and a lion breeding.*

I decided it was time to change the subject! The two-animal-breeding thing was not a concept I wanted to pursue, but it did bring up a lot of questions for future sessions.

REQUIREMENTS FOR
LIFE ON OTHER PLANETS

The more we discussed alien life, the more it was becoming apparent just how insignificant we were here on Earth. I thought I would pursue information about what common threads were needed to support life throughout the galaxy. His reply was quite interesting.

> *All need a fluid like water and a temperature moderate. And the planet must have gravity. And it must circulate, like have wind and tides. Have a good atmosphere to hold life.*

That all seemed to make sense. At least he finally made a statement that I could understand. In order to support life, a planet needs gravity, a moderate climate, some type of a fluid-like water, and some type of an atmosphere. When I asked Mou what the atmosphere was like on his planet, he had said:

> *We breathe a nitrogen-rich gas and water is not like yours.*

Life on other planets has adapted to their conditions much as life here on Earth has evolved through various environmental changes. Just how different the various forms of life are became apparent one session when he brought some of his friends along to help answer some of my questions. He started out by saying:

> *Mou's Friends. I have help tonight. A Lbyn and Bmt is with me. They are from different places.*

Having no idea what a Lbyn and Bmt were, I asked who they were. He answered:

> *Your aids to write.*

There are definitely times that I need all the help I can get when I write and he obviously felt he had to bring in reinforcements. My next question stated the obvious: Are they aliens?

> *Yes.*

Next, I asked if they were from a planet other than the one he came from. He was quick to tell me:

> *Yes, they are from other galaxies. We are from the Milky Way.*
> *They are from places your scientists have not seen.*

Not only am I getting writing help from aliens in our galaxy, Mou is bringing in help from galaxies that have not even been seen by our astronomers! I followed up by asking him to describe his friends.

> *Right. They are dead. Ha, Ha, Ha. All look the same.*

I finally get to talk to an alien and he thinks he's a comedian! He continued:

> *When in bodies they were on four legs with*
> *hands with three fingers and two thumbs. Their heads*
> *were round. They had one eye and a small mouth. They*
> *have small brains because they use most of it.*

At this point of the interview I was once again thinking that just about anything was possible. I thought this would be a good time to ask him about different types of alien individuals. Whenever I see pictures of aliens, they usually look like what is referred to as "Reptilian Grays." When I asked if that was a type of alien he said:

> *Yes. Of course the shape changers look like you.*
> *The little whites you draw are one too. Yes. But there*
> *are the spider people and the blues as I am.*

From that statement, it seems as though what I thought were "Grays" are really "Little Whites." Since size really does matter, I asked him how tall the Grays stood. His answer once again caught me by surprise.

> *Oh, anywhere from 8 to 15 feet. They are from a place*
> *with less gravity so they are tall. Small shape changers*
> *are 3 feet to 5 feet because they have more gravity.*

I cannot imagine what a group photograph of all the different types of aliens would look like. Of all the descriptions, I think the one of the spider people might get the most attention.

TIME CAN BE FASTER OR SLOWER

During our sessions, I was wondering if he could see ahead in time. Could he see the future?

> *I am dead so I see all time because in essence it has already happened. In life I was a slave to time too. Time is on all places of life. Time is not the same though, some time is slower and some faster but time is in all places.*

If I told you I understand what he just said, I would be lying. I do know that when the guides give a prediction, the event usually comes to pass, but they can be wrong about the times of occurrence. It seems that time is very confusing on the other side, but it is everywhere in the galaxy. The slower and faster thing needs a little more research, but that is also for another day.

A common theme throughout this book has been the fervent attempts by the governments of the world to keep the presence of aliens a secret. I asked him the main reason governments are so emphatic about maintaining secrecy. His answer was pretty much as I expected.

> *Fears. Today people run on fear. In times before, the people saw us as good news. A visit from God. After we told we were not Gods, we still remained Gods or men from the Heavens. Look what occurred when on the radio a play came on and it was a play about aliens attacking. Just a play and people killed themselves. It was kind of a test to see what you might do. Well, we all know only the crazy believe in ghosts and aliens.*

He was referring to the Orson Welles radio show I discussed earlier. The more I communicate with Mou, the more I am amazed at his knowledge and abilities. One evening I asked him if there was anything he could not do. Once again his response was not what I expected.

> *Eat onions.*

Apparently, when he was on Earth he'd tried some of our native foods. I asked him if he really did try to eat onions and he responded:

> *I did. It hurts.*

This chapter has been a plethora of information about our neighbors that occupy the Milky Way and beyond. After hours of contact with Mou, the alien spirit, I can tell you that many of his statements have proven correct.

One evening I asked Mou if he had but one message to tell the humans here on Earth, what would that message be? His answer was:

We are only here to help you. Just because you do not see us does not mean we are not here. There are many things you do not see that are around you. We are one of them and in fact we walk among you.

I liked that answer so much I used it for the Epigraph of this book. We discussed many other subjects with my newfound alien friend but that will be the subject of another book. After all, he stated earlier that he wanted to write two more.

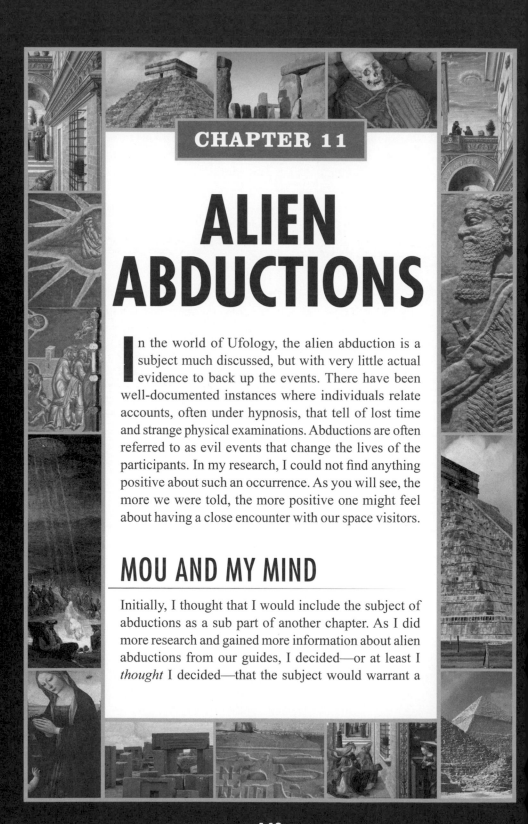

CHAPTER 11

ALIEN ABDUCTIONS

In the world of Ufology, the alien abduction is a subject much discussed, but with very little actual evidence to back up the events. There have been well-documented instances where individuals relate accounts, often under hypnosis, that tell of lost time and strange physical examinations. Abductions are often referred to as evil events that change the lives of the participants. In my research, I could not find anything positive about such an occurrence. As you will see, the more we were told, the more positive one might feel about having a close encounter with our space visitors.

MOU AND MY MIND

Initially, I thought that I would include the subject of abductions as a sub part of another chapter. As I did more research and gained more information about alien abductions from our guides, I decided—or at least I *thought* I decided—that the subject would warrant a chapter of its own. Since meeting Mou, I am not sure if the ideas coming into my head are my own or his. If you recall, he was quite clear about being able to enter my mind. When I asked if the idea of a separate chapter was mine, he replied:

Yeah, sure, ha, ha, ha.

A bit facetious, that was kind of the answer I expected from my spirit friend. Whenever I work on this book, there is no doubt in my mind that there is unsolicited help to what I type. You are about to find out, there is a lot more to abductions by extraterrestrials than ever imagined.

A REAL ABDUCTION

One of the most famous alien abduction stories took place in September 1961 in the State of New Hampshire. The story of Betty and Barney Hill is one of the most publicized abduction incidents in the world of Ufology.

Barney was a thirty-nine-year-old African-American male and his wife Betty was a forty-one-year-old white woman. Barney was employed by the postal service and his wife worked as a supervisor for child welfare. They were driving through a relatively isolated area in New Hampshire, returning from a vacation in Canada, when they saw what they believed was a bright star that was moving quite erratically in the sky.

They stopped the car and Barney got out to take a better look at the erratically moving light. Taking out a pair of binoculars and observing the object, he realized that it was definitely not a star. What he observed was a strange flying craft with different colored lights and rows of windows through which he could observe individuals moving around. He could not make out if the craft was inhabited by humans.

Alarmed at what they were watching, Barney and Betty attempted to flee by speeding away from the ship. They were not aware of any events taking place or lapses in time. All they knew was that the UFO was no longer in sight. As they drove on, they suddenly realized that they were thirty-five miles down the road from where they'd stopped to observe the flying object. Unaware of any physical changes, they continued the drive to their home with no further incidents.

The couple was troubled by what they had seen. At the urging of family members, Betty contacted the military at Pease Air Force Base and reported what they had seen to Major Paul W. Henderson. They were shocked to hear from the major that a UFO had been confirmed on their radar. The couple returned home and attempted to put the incident behind them. Unfortunately, Betty began to have nightmares in which she and her husband were being forced to enter a strange type of aircraft. When they recreated a time line for the evening of the encounter, it became obvious that they had lost two hours of time during the incident. Something had happened—they simply did not know the details of what had taken place during the time lapse.

In an attempt to learn what had occurred, the couple contacted Dr. Benjamin Simon, a well-regarded psychiatrist and neurologist from Boston. In an attempt to reconstruct the missing events that took place during the lost two hours, the Doctor used regressive hypnosis, a treatment that can be effective in recovering lost memories. After extensive study, the Doctor came to the conclusion the couple had been abducted and taken aboard some type of a craft.

While under hypnosis they revealed that their automobile had stalled on the road. As soon as the automobile came to a stop, the UFO landed on the road and several aliens got out of the ship and approached their car. They carried the couple to the ships where certain tests were conducted. Among the procedures performed were skin sampling, mental tests, and samples of nails, hair, and skin. Gynecological testing was performed on Betty and sperm samples were taken from Barney. Hypnosis was performed on the couple to erase their memories and they were told not to disclose their abduction to anyone.

Under the regression hypnosis they described the perpetrators as "bald-headed alien beings, about five foot tall, with greyish skin, pear-shaped heads and slanting cat-like eyes." (Keep in mind that these are the findings of a very reputable doctor.) It certainly appears that quite a bit happened to the couple during the lost two hours. This famous case is considered one of the best-recorded instances of an abduction. It also gives insight into what actually occurred during their visits on the alien ships.

The aliens described by the Hills are what Ufologists refer to as the "Greys" (also spelled Grays). Chapter 3, Ancient Aliens, include paintings on walls of caves that include images of this type of alien. When I inquired if the Greys were dangerous to humans, the guide answered:

If not ruled by the council they would
take over many places like your earth.

Reptilian Grays seem to be some of the more aggressive types of aliens performing abductions. We can all be thankful the galaxy has a strong governing system.

A LOT OF ABDUCTIONS

Thanks to television shows and the movies, if there is one thing that creates fear among humans, it is the thought of being taken against your will by extraterrestrials and being used for biological testing. When I asked him how many abductions take place each year, his answer left no doubt to the scope of the happenings.

Oh my, thousands.

My research shows that alien abductions are not just an American phenomenon. His answer to the extent of the extraterrestrial research projects was:

Worldwide.

At this point, we know that there are thousands of abductions a year taking place all around the world. I thought it would be good to understand if our alien friend had participated in any human abductions. I was pleased to hear his answer...I think.

Me, no, but the ship I was on, yes.

At least he wasn't a direct participant, but I would certainly think he knows what takes place during such events from personal experience.

THE PURPOSE OF ALIEN ABDUCTIONS

I asked Mou why people from all parts of the galaxy came to earth to study humans and the purpose of the studies. His reply pointed out the abductions had a positive intent.

They do this to advance mankind, not to cause harm. We have aided in many ways from your beginning. Your sciences did not put mankind on earth soon enough. They are some 50,000 years later.

My alien friend was quite emphatic that this message be included in this book. He wants everyone to realize that, in spite of all the bad publicity, the research conducted on humans is for their own good. As if to reiterate his point he said the following:

*There are many studies. There will be one on this new
breakout of the virus to see if they can stop it through
genes or the like. The same way Salk stopped polio.*

As I was writing this book, we were in the first throes of Ebola in the United States. Our friends on the other side are quite concerned and it appears were conducting tests in an attempt to find a cure. From this statement, it also appears that aliens assisted in the research that helped cure polio. I can remember from my biology classes that we learned a lot of information from dissecting various things. I asked him if they ever dissected humans.

*Never living. We have machines to do that. This is where your
MRI machines come from. But interesting, if we find things like
cancer in a person we cure it before sending them back.*

I made a mental note to find out why aliens have an immediate cure for cancer, but doctors here on Earth don't. It was starting to appear like an awful lot of our technologies were given to us by the more advanced cultures from outer space.

SELECTED FOR STUDY

I thought it would be interesting to pursue what process the aliens go through in selecting candidates for abduction. When I asked Mou how people are selected for study, his answer was quite lengthy and candid.

*They watch a group of people. Say a college,
and they know what tests they are doing. They exclude
people with the abilities to remember their dreams. They
pick the people who can be hypnotized and then they pick
out body types. They then pick people that live alone.
Like those who live alone and do not see others.*

I asked him if the people were ever not returned after an abduction. His answer was kind of comforting.

No, that is the law on tests.

Apparently, the galactic governing committee has strict rules dictating what can and cannot be currently performed on humans. It seems as though the rules were a lot more lax in the past. The book *Alien Agenda* by Jim Marrs suggests that the current outbreak of autism can be attributed to alien abductions in the past where they performed experiments on human genes. He also suggested that the Grays did gene experiments to give humans more longevity. His answer was:

> *He was correct on the experiment in gene purpose.*
> *He is wrong the grays wanted to see how mixing their*
> *genes with yours would give them a bigger brain and would*
> *give you a longer DNA string letting you live longer and*
> *change so you could space travel. The first generation*
> *was ok but the next was the trouble, causing autism.*

K and Doc have a nephew with autism. They asked who was abducted who would have caused the problem with their nephew. Mou's answer was:

> *It would be the great grandparents. Those of the*
> *creators of what you call baby boomers. Most were military,*
> *GI's. Put that in your book. I am not of the greys.*

This was the first time I heard about the relationship between aliens and autism. It seems as though our greatest generation was also the subject of experimentation that would create the current outbreak of autism. When I asked if that type of experimentation was still allowed, he replied:

> *What was done in the past is no longer permitted.*

That is certainly good news. Unfortunately, there is a generation of young people suffering from autism as a result of alien experimentation.

WHAT REALLY HAPPENS

During one of our channeling sessions, I asked what happens to humans when they are involved in an abduction. He replied:

> *We take them to a lab. We do tests on DNA.*
> *If they are ill they are repaired and taken back. Most*
> *do not recall. Less than 10% remember something.*

When you say the abductees' illnesses are repaired, you insinuate you have a cure for cancer. Have you tried to share the cure with humans?

You have it, but money is better to you. It is easy. Add oxygen.

I had always heard that drug companies would rather treat an illness than cure it. Cancer research is certainly big business. Since Mou said that only a few of the victims of abductions can remember what happened, I asked him if aliens can control the minds of humans.

Kind of, but not really. More tune into thoughts.

I can tell you from personal experience that guides have no trouble tuning into thoughts. Whenever I make up questions concerning a subject, the guides come prepared to answer them. I followed up by saying that aliens could read minds, but not control them. His answer was:

Right, control is hard.

Note that he said mind control is hard—not impossible. If there are thousands of people being studied, there must be an awful lot of information being gathered. I asked him what they did with all the information that was being collected through their studies on humans.

*It is put into our computers and analyzed.
Compiled and a study written.*

When I asked him who received the information that was compiled during an abduction he answered:

The planet doing it, the committee, and the government.

Notice the "and the government" part of his answer. I went on to ask him if the aliens are communicating with our government. His answer did not come as a surprise.

Yes.

SURGICAL IMPLANTS

The stories of alien abductions are all over the Internet. The other evening I was watching a documentary about a surgeon that specialized in removing small implants that were deposited in the bodies of abduction victims. When removed, the implants seemed to be small meteorite particles. Tests showed them to be inert and the scientists could not determine the purpose of the small foreign object in the bodies of the victims. One amazing feature of the implants was that there was no evidence of an incision on the skin of the victims.

Next, I inquired if the extraterrestrials place implants in the bodies of their victims. His answer was:

Yes.

What is the purpose of the implants? His one word answer was:

Programming.

My next comment was more of a statement than a question: the implants look like meteorite material.

Yes.

The idea of the implants seemed quite interesting. When I asked the purpose of the implants, our alien guide replied:

Only a few get these. It is a radio transmitter for study.

According to our spirit sources, alien abductions have a very positive effect on the human race. We have been told that information extracted from involuntary subjects has contributed to vaccines that have cured polio and given us technology similar our MRI machines. Gene testing that was allowed in the past and led to the current proliferation of autism has been eliminated by the galactic governing committee.

My interviews with Mou have been quite informative as we investigated many areas where extraterrestrials have affected our planet. Hopefully, the information has contributed to ending some of the myths about what really happens when humans and aliens interact. When I started this chapter, I had no idea how hard the visitors from outer space work to contribute to the advancement of the human race. He has also given insight into just how advanced the visitors from outer space really are as they have saved humans from themselves. I suspect that mankind would still be in the Stone Age without the help of the alien visitors.

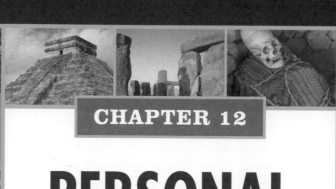

CHAPTER 12

PERSONAL ENCOUNTERS

I f by now you still don't believe in extraterrestrials, you probably won't think that I've actually had personal interactions with aliens. My guess also is that many of you think I am firmly in the nut-job category. As you will see, what I photographed is not what you would expect from the vast library of alien photographs on the Internet. There is no logical explanation for the photographs you are about to see. If you have a suggestion other than aliens, please feel free to contact me and let me know what the subject matter is in the pictures. There is also a segment in this chapter where I tell the story of getting a glimpse of the blue-skinned alien spirit with whom we have been communicating through our channeling sessions and how he verified the sighting.

While I was writing my first book, *Haunting and History of the Battle of Gettysburg*, I spent many hours on the Gettysburg battlefield, by myself, taking digital pictures. In fact, I took over 60,000 photographs, many of which showed the paranormal activity for which the

area is so famous. At the time, I just figured the strange images were spirit interactions. According to the master guides, there was a little more to what I was observing than I'd expected.

ACTIVITY ON THE GETTYSBURG WHEAT FIELD

Lights in the sky taken over the Gettysburg battlefield. Courtesy author.

For those of you not familiar with the battle of the wheat field at Gettysburg, on the second day of fighting, the Union and Confederate forces fought some of the most brutal combat of the entire campaign at this location. It is estimated that the eight acres of the wheat field accounted for 6,000 casualties. It is one of the most spiritually active areas, and I spent a lot of time photographing on that hallowed ground.

While I consider myself an expert in paranormal photography, one evening in 2011, I photographed a series of images that were quite unique and something that I was unable to explain. The foreground of the image shows the monument dedicated to the New York Light Artillery that fought in this location. The camera I was using at the time was set at a shutter speed of 1/60th of a second. The implication of this camera setting is that any object leaving a trail similar to an object in a timed exposure would have to move very fast. You will also see that the monument in the foreground is in perfect focus, so I was not moving the camera. The image in the sky is approximately 300 yards from my position and looks like a moving subject in a timed exposure. As you can see, there was some type of a light-emitting object that was moving very rapidly in the evening sky.

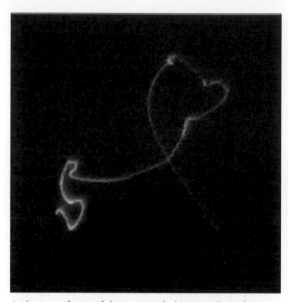

A close-up of one of the strange lights over Gettysburg. The image was taken at a shutter speed of 1/60 of a second. Courtesy author.

During the course of that evening, I photographed eight frames that showed the trail of the rapidly moving objects. In the picture on the left, you can see what I believe was the most impressive photograph of the series. Whatever was creating the image, it was moving very rapidly and some-what erratic. (Keep in mind all the movement had to take place in 1/60th of a second.) Whatever it was, the object certainly looked like it was having a hard time making up its mind where it wanted to go. Adding to the mystery, I could not see the object with my eyes, only on the back screen of the camera in the finished photograph. It is quite possible I did not see the objects because they were only visible during the split second the shutter was open on the camera. These are the images that I discussed in the chapter concerning the Rendlesham Forest Lights.

MYSTERY OBJECT IN THE SLAUGHTER PEN

Several months later, in September 2011, I was on the battlefield taking photographs. The last thing on my mind was mysterious flying objects. A great night for paranormal photography, the weather was very warm and humid. It is my belief that the humidity adds energy to the air, often allowing ectoplasm or energy mist to form. This night I was feeling lazy, so I had borrowed my wife's convertible, put the top down, and was driving around the different areas of the National Park, taking pictures from the car and looking for activity.

I decided to drive through an area along a small creek named Plumb Run that ran through a low-lying area called the Slaughter Pen. On the second day of the battle at Gettysburg, so many men were killed in this area along the creek that the area earned its name. As the wounded and dying crawled to the creek for a last drink, the water actually ran red with the blood of the soldiers.

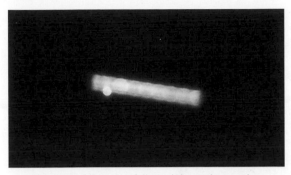

A strange bar of light that followed the author on the Gettysburg battlefield. The round object is the moon. Courtesy author.

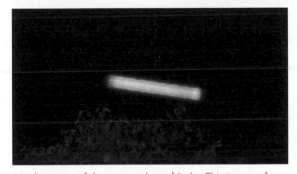

Another view of the strange bar of light. This is one of approximately forty separate photographs taken of the strange light. Courtesy author.

There are places to pull off along the road in this area, so I decided to stop and take some pictures without getting out of the car. On this particular evening I was using three cameras on a light bar so I could rapidly take multiple frames if I came across some vigorous spirit activity.

When I took the first picture and looked at the back screen, there was a line of bluish light like nothing I had ever viewed before. At first glance, I figured my camera had malfunctioned. I took a picture with the second camera and the same light, in a slightly different position, appeared. Camera number three had the same image. Whatever was appearing, it was on all of my photographic equipment. At this point, I began taking a lot of frames!

The picture of the light bar above was one of the first images of the evening. If you look closely, you will see a round light in the lower left corner. It just happened that the moon lined up with the image. Not part of the activity, but a good point of reference as to the size of the object. As I was snapping the images, I had absolutely no idea what seemed to be posing for my pictures.

When you are alone at night at one of the most haunted areas in the country, some strange thoughts sometimes start to enter your mind. While extraterrestrials were not on my mind when I pulled off the road, the thought suddenly started to occur to me that there might be a little more to what was taking place in front of me. In response to the not overly comforting idea, I pulled the car back on to the road and started to drive slowly, taking pictures as I drove. I wasn't real pleased when the object kept pace with my car—like I was being followed!

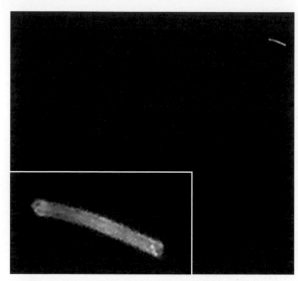

Another light bar taken in a separate incident.
Courtesy author.

During this period of time I was snapping pictures out the side of the car. By the time the object stopped following me, I'd taken over fifty frames on all three of the cameras that verified the presence of the mysterious light bar. As I drove down the road, I must admit that the speed of my vehicle increased. When I entered the Devil's Den area, the bar of light stopped following me and disappeared from sight. The incident was a bit unnerving as thoughts of alien abductions began to enter my mind. The most comforting thought I could come up with was there was no way my butt was going to fit in that little light bar.

For the next year I used the photographs in my lectures, but always just referred to them as unknown objects. Little did I know that the mysterious light bars would appear to me again, almost twelve months after the first experience in the Slaughter Pen.

IT'S BACK!!

By September 2012, I needed a few more pictures of spirit activity to finish my research. Once again it was a warm and humid evening and I was photographing in the Wheat Field. When I went back to the apartment that night and reviewed the photographs for the evening, I realized there was a familiar image. I had recorded another image of our light bar visitor!

The above image shows the close up of the mysterious lights. Note the similarity from the pictures taken a year earlier. Whatever was creating the lights, it certainly was not bashful.

After the second sighting I realized that whatever was appearing to me was not an accident. In earlier sessions with the guides, I had been told that aliens observe and report back. I wasn't particularly happy with the concept that visitors from outer space were observing yours truly. It was time to ask the guides what was happening.

THE GUIDES EXPLAIN

During our next private channeling session we had the master guide named Philip answer questions about aliens. I asked him if the light bars I had photographed were the work of extraterrestrials. His reply was:

*May have been. You need to understand
that these beings watch and report.*

Great. Now I have to keep looking over my shoulder when I am on the battlefield. I asked the guide if I was being specifically watched and reported on. I breathed a sigh of relief when his answer was:

No.

Next, I inquired if it was possible for humans to initiate contact with aliens. He answered:

Not at will.

You can rest assured I have no intent of initiating contact! Just for good measure I asked if there was any risk for humans to initiate contact. His reply was what I kind of expected.

There can be.

I made a mental note to never initiate contact with live aliens. At the time it never occurred to me that I would be able to communicate with the spirit of an alien on a regular basis.

ANOTHER PERSONAL ENCOUNTER

The story of the light bar does not quite end there. In April 2014, I was doing a book signing at the annual Phenomacon Convention in Gettysburg. The exhibitors included some of the most talented psychics and paranormal investigators in the country. While talking with one of the exhibitors, the conversation came up about alien encounters.

I'd mentioned to him that I had been followed by a mysterious light bar on the Gettysburg battlefield and was actually able to take multiple pictures of the object. When I described the object, his eyes lit up. He mentioned that when he was a child he had an encounter with an object much like what I had just described. When he made a pencil sketch of what he had seen, it looked an awful lot like what I had photographed.

When I took him back to my table and showed him the actual pictures, his eyes really lit up. He said the object was exactly what he had observed as a child! He went on to say that as he became more experienced in the alien and paranormal field, his belief became that the light bar was actually some type of an observation drone. This explanation makes a lot of sense in light of the guide's statement that the extraterrestrials observe and report back. I do know that the light bar I photographed observed me for as long as ten minutes that night in 2012. I have no idea if it reported back to anyone.

CONNIE'S ABDUCTION

I think I mentioned earlier that sometimes events take place in your lives that do not seem to have much significance at the time but turn out to be quite important. During the 1990s we lived in south Florida to be near our young grandchildren. I had to fly out of town on business, so Connie dropped me off at the Ft. Lauderdale airport. As she was driving back alone on I-95, one of the most heavily traveled highways in the country, she blacked out and lost all conscious memory. About fifteen minutes later, it was as if someone pushed a button and she became totally aware of her surroundings. What Connie immediately realized was that she was approximately twenty miles and two exits north of where she'd lost consciousness!

By some means she had managed to travel over twenty miles in heavy traffic without having an accident or having any memory of the events. Upon telling me what happened, I insisted she go immediately to our doctor. She had numerous tests, including having to wear a heart monitor. The doctor's conclusion was that he had no idea what had occurred, but there was no evidence of a physical event explaining the period of memory loss. He also said the she must have just fallen asleep. Not many people sleep while driving twenty miles on I-95 without getting killed. Whatever happened, the cause of the incident remained a mystery.

During a channeling session with Mou at Golden Lane one evening in 2015, we were investigating what took place during an alien abduction. As the questioning progressed, it became apparent that many people were abducted who had no memory of the journeys. When I asked if Connie had ever been abducted, I was caught off guard when he answered:

Yes.

Not exactly the answer we were expecting, but I *have* accused her of being a little spacey at times. She immediately asked if the abduction happened during her ride on I-95 in Florida. Once again the answer was:

Yes.

The mystery of her little trip was solved! She'd apparently seen the inside of a UFO but had no memory. We did not pursue the details of her abduction on that evening, but the opportunity for additional questioning would arise again.

That time came in July of 2015 when Mou appeared for us in a channeling session with K and Doc in Park City, Utah. There were several guests listening to the answers and there were a few cocktails present. I asked my friend what happened when Connie was abducted.

I was not there. I am innocent. I am having a drink with everyone.

I should have asked how a spirit can have a drink with everyone. Judging from that answer, I realized there was going to be very few details of what took place on this evening. I inquired how they kept the car on the road for that twenty miles if Connie was not driving. His answer gave an indication of just what the alien community is capable of.

Someone drove for her. It is easy when you know how.

It might be easy for an alien, but I still wanted to know what happened. I reworded the question. "Who drove for her?"

Shape shifter. What is nice is we never get driving tickets. We turn off cars. We steal their energy.

They'd abducted Connie, put a shape shifter that looked like a human in the driver seat, drove for twenty miles, put her back in the seat and never got a driving ticket. On top of that, they erased all of her memory of the event. That is one hell of an accomplishment!

As time progresses, he still will not disclose what happened while Connie enjoyed the hospitality of our alien friends. As far as I can tell she has suffered no long-term problems, but, as with all events that happen in our lives, there is always a reason.

A VERY PERSONAL CONTACT

How many of you can say you have actually seen an alien, or in this case, an alien spirit? Since we began channeling by Skype with K and Doc in Salt Lake City, our information concerning our alien neighbors seemed to be growing by the day. With Mou's help, I had written the closing chapter for this book and the words had come to me quite easily. When Connie read the first draft she commented that I had moved my writing up a notch. I told her that I was sure I had help from my blue-skinned friend.

The morning after I wrote the closing chapter, we both woke up early and decided to go to a local restaurant for breakfast. Still excited about how the book was coming along, we discussed our conversations with Mou and how amazing it was to be chosen for this information path. As we were talking, out of the corner of my eye, I saw a blue flash coming from the chair next to me. I immediately told Connie that I thought I'd just gotten a glimpse of the blue alien. Needless to say, I was quite careful to make sure no one at a nearby table overheard that comment! Mentally I made a note to make sure to ask him if I was starting to imagine things or he had really decided to visit New Oxford, Pennsylvania.

Several days later, it was time to once again do a long-distance channeling session with our friends. We started by Doc asking if Mou was present and if he had a message. His first unsolicited comment left no doubt that he'd decided to have breakfast with us. He started by saying:

Hi from the blue flash.

Without any hesitation or prompting he let us know that he really had appeared to me as the blue flash I'd witnessed during breakfast several days earlier! Not only am I now seeing human spirits and angels, extraterrestrial spirits are also making their presence known. His follow-up statement also let me know just how close he was when I was writing the other night:

The book turned out great. Better than expected.
You are a better writer than me.

Did I mention that flattery will get everything? I asked if he had been helping me transcribe the notes and work on this book. His answer reaffirmed my suspicions.

Yes, your vocabulary is much better than mine.

I tried to reiterate that he really had the ability to enter my mind and influence what I was writing. Again he said something he'd said at another meeting:

And enjoying your mind too. I was.

He had said he could get into my eyes and see what I write. It was becoming obvious Mou really wasn't kidding. Since that time there have been many instances where he assisted in helping me with this book. In another session he signed in with:

*Now to the book. You need to add a bit to a few
chapters. You are lacking explanation. You are going to
leave the readers on a cliff if you do not add a few
sentences to explain your conclusions. Skim through
it and I will point out what I am saying.*

When I went back to review the chapters, it was like I was led to which ones needed additional work. He was right; there were chapters that left the reader hanging and this chapter was one of them. He must approve of what changes I've made since my nose did not tickle or my eyes get blurry vision when I made the changes. In the last channeling session before I sent the book to the publisher, I asked him if he thought any other changes should be made. His reply was:

I read it and it is good. I am happy.

SMILE FOR THE CAMERA

During another later session, I thought it would be a good idea to include a picture of my blue-skinned friend in this book. It never occurred to me that I might have already taken a photograph of him at an earlier time. When I asked Mou if he would appear to me so I could take his picture he replied:

*Well now, I already have two times. Right. Look at
past film. Blue like streak. Look, thumb thru things.*

Mou, the blue flash. Courtesy author.

The next day I started to go through picture files but could not figure out what image he was referring to. Connie saw what I was doing and told me to look at one of the images I was using in my lectures. The picture she referred to was a strange blue streak of light that I had included in my list of images of unknown origin, taken on the Gettysburg battlefield nearly four years earlier. Whenever I conducted one of my lectures, I referred to the photograph as an unknown spirit light.

While I was looking through the photographs, I ran across a couple of other images that might also have been my blue friend. The next time we channeled, I thought it would be a good idea to play it safe and ask him to verify I was using the proper image. When I asked him if the image Connie had pointed out was the right one, he replied:

Yes, it is a grand likeness of me.

Not much modesty there! I jokingly asked him if he would like a copy of the picture and he replied:

All the lady blue streaks would be jealous. Ha, ha, ha. Your photos would be streaked.

Once again, Mou's sense of humor come shining through. I can only guess what he meant by saying the photos would be streaked.. Not only had the blue streak appeared for a photograph, he'd done it years before I'd ever thought about writing a book about aliens. It has become obvious that this book was preordained for a considerable time by spirit guides of this Earth and our galaxy. The more I learn, the more I am amazed at the miracles of our world around us.

My personal encounters with Mou continue as he gives me additional information concerning the visitors from other planets that are among us. We are already working on my future books that will shed even more light on our world around us. The fact that he enjoys my mind still is beyond Connie's comprehension.

CHAPTER 13

A GALACTIC OVERVIEW

Gathering the information presented in this book has been a life-changing epiphany for those of us involved with channeling the information from the other side of the life veil. When I started to write, it never occurred to me that aliens had eternal souls that resided in a universal Heaven under the control of a supreme God. In my wildest imagination it also never occurred to me that it would be possible to communicate with alien spirits in the same manner as when we communicated with human spirits and heavenly guides.

THE GIFT OF ALIEN COMMUNICATION

In the beginning of our quest for information about visitors from outer space, our guides cooperated in answering questions. Access to information expanded greatly when we were introduced to Mou. He introduced us to concepts and information that would have never occurred to me under ordinary circumstance. As I look back on the events that formed the foundation for this book, I now understand how my guides led me down the path of learning.

When starting, I'd never realized how small a part the human race plays in the overall picture of life in our galaxy and beyond. When I thought about aliens, it was always humans trying to determine if there was life on other planets in our Solar System and beyond. While we look for micro-organisms on Mars, there are advanced species in our backyard watching us look for life on other planets.

It never occurred to me that we might be a microscopically small fish in an ocean of planets and Solar Systems that supported life. Equally incomprehensible was the fact that life on Earth is at a very early stage of growth compared to other galactic cultures. In reality, human superiority might be an imagined myth not shared by any other intergalactic species.

Compound that thought with the concept that our species is at such an early and violent stage of our development, that visitors from other planets would come here to study the characteristics of human life. In their eyes, Earth might be the "Club Med of the Galaxy" where they can come to watch humans fight, much like the gladiators of Rome—a place to observe the human species in their habitat and report back to their superiors. Their actions are much the same as humans visiting a zoo to try to understand the habits of animals in a cage.

A GALACTIC GOVERNING COMMITTEE

It also never occurred to me that life on other planets would be so advanced that the members of the galaxy learned the stupidity of killing each other eons ago and formed a governing committee that controlled the actions of galactic residents: a veritable Galactic United Nations, only this organization functions with efficiency and rules are obeyed by all.

This committee protects underdeveloped planets, like Earth, from having the superior or more-advanced visitors from other worlds interfere with humans' natural development. If would-be visitors have a bad criminal record or evil intentions, they are not given permission to observe the fledgling human population. Visitors to Earth are only allowed to observe and not intervene or influence events that determine history. If the visitors want to mess with humans, they are allowed to create crop circles and watch how the earthlings react. That is probably always good for a laugh from our intergalactic neighbors.

God even gave the human residents of Earth very short longevity so they could only make so many mistakes in a lifetime. Other kinder and wiser cultures in the Milky Way were given lifetimes up to 1,000 years. You can acquire a lot of wisdom in 1,000 years! Unfortunately, governments here on Earth don't want their people to acquire any of that knowledge and go to great extremes to keep the information from the people. It is like a line spoken in the 1992 movie *A Few Good Men* when Col. Jessep says: "You can't handle the truth."

When it comes to travel, humans finally learned to move around the earth in automobiles or fly in planes at relatively slow speeds. More advanced cultures can ride energy waves that travel faster than the speed of light, causing time to move in reverse. Their energy travels so rapidly that they can go from the farthest part of the Milky Way to Earth in less than a day if conditions are right. They can even time travel back from the future if necessary.

IF AT FIRST YOU DON'T SUCCEED, REINCARNATE

Like more advanced cultures, the human species is given the opportunity to reincarnate, so they can return to an incarnate life. This act gives them the opportunity to attempt to educate their souls so they can advance in the realms of Heaven. Since they are such slow learners, humans have to reincarnate many times because their free will lets them do things that are inherently stupid—like poisoning the air they breathe. God even sent his own son to Earth to provide guidance, but because of the free-will thing, over half the population came to ignore his preachings. Needless to say, the Supreme Being is a bit upset over this. Visitors from outer space have an awful lot to observe on Earth. No wonder motherships carry 200 people; they are probably tourists looking for a good laugh.

The preceding narrative seems very far fetched, but guess what? According to our conversations with Mou, and other spirits acting as channeling guides, those paragraphs are a pretty accurate depiction of what takes place in our galaxy. Alien visitors have been visiting Earth since the time of the dinosaurs and have been keeping a close eye on Earth and its residents for a very long time. They do indeed seem to be the watchdogs of the universe.

Major governments of the world have attempted to hide the evidence of the existence of extraterrestrials, in spite of volumes of data to the contrary. The standard excuse is that the knowledge would cause panic through the people of the world. Men in Black from many countries prevailed in keeping dirty little secrets about aliens from the folks. It never occurred to them that if the truth were known about aliens, many people might take comfort in the fact that we are being protected from negative interplanetary forces. People might even demand they be protected from the bad forces of our own governments.

PROOF OF ALIENS

In this book, I've presented multiple pieces of evidence of the existence of ancient aliens and attempted to explain what took place when those early civilizations came into contact with alien visitors. You may have been surprised to find out that there were many references to alien events in the Holy Bible. After all, as we found out, aliens are God's creatures and, in many instances, my belief is that he thinks a lot more of them than he does of humans. He certainly gave them a head start in their development over us.

Major alien events were investigated and I've attempted to present them in a factual manner. Questions were then asked of the guides to compare what actually happened with the historical documentation and official stories surrounding alien sightings. Our guides gave us detailed answers concerning events of such importance as Roswell and Rendlesham Forest. As you can see, the official version of the events differ greatly from what apparently really took place.

It is quite obvious to me that the visitors from outer space now think that it is time for their story to be told. I have no clue why they have selected me as a conduit for the storytelling, but I am honored and hope this accounting meets their expectations. Mou has told us that he has plans for two more books. My guess is that when he is ready, I will learn what he has in mind.

One evening we were having a session and it dawned on me that a lot of the information my alien friend was giving to me had gotten people prematurely terminated and in need of reincarnation. Many of the things in this book, to the best of my knowledge have never appeared in print. In fact, some of the information caused me some concern for my safety. When I asked him if I could print this information without getting killed, he replied:

I am giving you things that are safe. You ask me questions.
I dumb down for your safety. You are just another nut job.

Unfortunately, he just verified what my daughters think about my writing. After the "dumb down" statement, I think he deserves at least one snide remark, so here goes: "You would think that a species that could cure cancer could eat an onion." I guess everyone has their weaknesses.

As we closed out the session I mentioned to Connie how amazing the path was that God had chosen for us.

ENDNOTES

Chapter 5

1. www.ufowevidence.org.
2. www.ufosightingsdaily.com.
3. www.jamesoberg.com.
4. www.syti.net.
5. www.syti.com.
6. ronrecord.com.
7. www.ufocasebook.com.
8. *Alien Interview*, edited by Lawrence R. Spencer. www.Lulu.com, 2011.
9. www.geocaching.com/geocache/GC1H6HM_the-jimmy-carter-ufo-incident?guid=e5f9871d-476e-4977-b327-a21e20d7d33c.
10. Twichell, David E. *Global Implications of the UFO Reality*, p79, Infinity, 2003
11. Waring, Scott. *UFO Sightings of 2006–2009*. p120, I Universe, Bloomington, IN, 2010.
12. Waring, Scott. *UFO Sightings of 2006–2009*. p121, I Universe, Bloomington, IN, 2010.
13. www.regan.utexas.edu. Address to the 42nd Session of the United Nations, September 21, 1987.

Chapter 8

1. Warren, Larry and Peter Robbins, *Left at East Gate*, Cosimo Books, New York, 1997.

BIBLIOGRAPHY

Books

Berliner, Don and Stanton T. Friedman. *Crash at Corona: The U.S. Military Retrieval and Cover-Up of a UFO.* Paraview, 2012.

Corso, Col. Philip J. *The Day After Roswell.* New York: Simon & Schuster, 1998.

Pope, Nick. *Encounters in Rendlesham Forest.* New York: St. Martins, 2015.

Marrs, Jim. *Alien Agenda.* New York: Harper Collins, 2000.

Randle, Kevin D. *Invasion Washington.* New York: Harper Collins, 2001.

Stitchin, Zecharia. *The 12th Planet.* New York: Stein and Day, 2007.

Strohm, Barry. *Afterlife, What Really Happens on the Other Side*, Schiffer, Atglen, PA, 2013.

Strohm, Barry, *Haunting and History of the Battle of Gettysburg.* Gettysburg, PA: Thomas, 2010.

Twitchell, David E. *Global Implication of the UFO Reality.* Infinity, 2003.

Waring, Scott. *UFO Sightings 2006–2009.* I Universe, Bloomington, IN, 2010.

Warren, Larry and Peter Robbins. *Left at East Gate.* New York: Cosimo Books, 1997.

Websites

After Disclosure. www.afterdisclosure.com

Alieneight.com. http://alieneight.com

Aliens Were Here. www.alienswerehere.com/AncientAlienEvidence.html

Astronauts Lovell & Borman. http://ronrecord.com/astronauts/lovell-borman.html

Cosmic Search Magazine. www.bigear.org/vol1no1/kraus1.htm

David Clark, New Light on Rendlesham. http://drdavidclarke.co.uk/secret-files/secret-files-4

English Heritage.org. www.english-heritage.org.uk

Geocaching. http://www.geocaching.com/geocache/GC1H6HM_the-jimmy-carter-ufo-incident?guid=e5f9871d-476e-4977-b327-a21e20d7d33c

James O. Berg.com. www.jamesoberg.com

Six Most Famous Alien Sightings.

www.switched.com/2009/06/20/the-6-most-famous-ufo-sightings-in-history

Ron Record.com. ronrecord.com/astronauts/armstrong-collins-aldrin.html

Syti.Ne. www.syti.net

Lightside.org. www.thelightside.org/EARSite/ears_ufos_biblefiles1.html

Twenty Famous UFO Sightings. www.stylist.co.uk/life/20-famous-ufo-extra-
    terrestrial-and-alien-sightings
ufocasebook.com. www.ufocasebook.com
UFO Evidence. www.ufoevidence.org/cases/case355.htm
UFO Sightings Daily. www.ufosightingdaily.com
University of Texas. www.regan.texas.edu
Address to the 42nd Session of the United Nations, September 21, 1987

OTHER SCHIFFER BOOKS BY THE AUTHOR

Afterlife What Really Happens on the Other Side
True Stories of Contact and Communication with Spirits
ISBN: 978-0-7643-4734-4

OTHER SCHIFFER BOOKS ON RELATED SUBJECTS

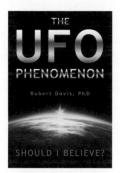

The UFO Phenomenon
Should I Believe?
Robert Davis.
ISBN: 978-0-7643-4764-1

UFO and Alien Management
A Guide to Discovering, Evaluating, and Directing Sightings, Abductions, and Contactee Experiences
Dinah Roseberry
ISBN: 978-0-7643-4606-4

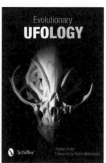

Evolutionary UFOlogy
Jordan Hoffer
ISBN: 978-0-7643-4505-0

"Tails" of the Afterlife
True Stories of Ghost Pets
Peggy Schmidt
ISBN: 978-0-7643-3253-1